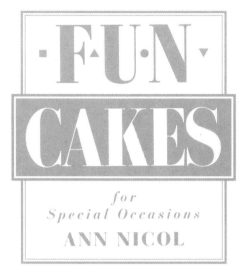

·F·U·N·
CAKES
for
Special Occasions
ANN NICOL

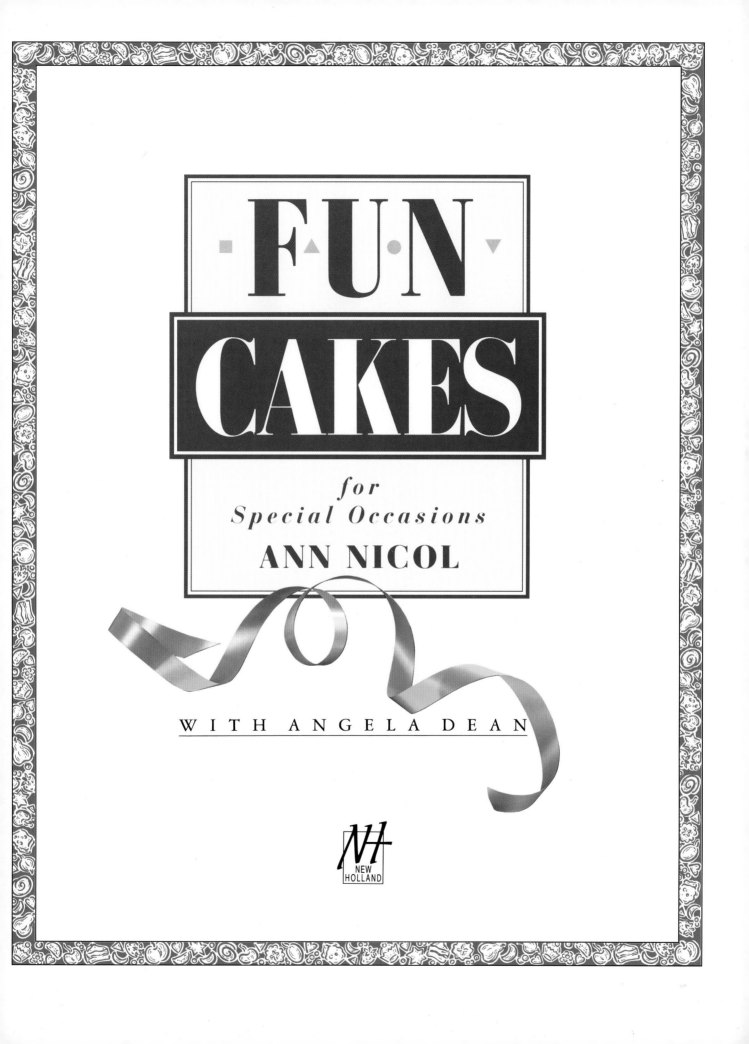

·F·U·N·
CAKES

for
Special Occasions

ANN NICOL

WITH ANGELA DEAN

NH
NEW
HOLLAND

First published in 1992
by Letts of London
an imprint of New Holland (Publishers) Ltd
London • Cape Town • Sydney • Singapore

24 Nutford Place
London W1H 6DQ
United Kingdom

80 McKenzie Street
Cape Town 8001
South Africa

3/2 Aquatic Drive
Frenchs Forest, NSW 2086
Australia

First published in paperback 1995

5 7 9 10 8 6 4

ISBN 1 85238 199 X (hardback)
ISBN 1 85368 586 O (paperback)

A CIP catalogue record for this book is available from the British Library

Editorial Director: Joanna Lorenz
Art Director: Peter Bridgewater
Project Editor: Judith Simons, Jennifer Jones
Jacket and styled photography: Chris Turner
Step-by-step photography: Leslie Kingsbury Wheeler
Home Economists: Ann Nicol, Angela Dean and Louise Pickford

Printed and bound in Singapore

CONTENTS

RECIPES AND TECHNIQUES

■ ● ▲

All the cakes in the book are based on three easy, basic recipes: a Quick Mix Sponge Cake, a Rich Fruit Cake (and a lighter variation, Light Apple Fruit Cake) and a Chocolate Cake. You will also find recipes for icings and fillings, almond paste, and sugarpaste, which is ideal for making dainty flowers and for modelling. The techniques cover all the basics of cake decorating, from covering a cake with almond paste and fondant icing, to lining tins and making your own piping bags. There is also a note on useful items of cake decorating equipment.

From top left: Slimmer's Lunch for One (page 36), Christmas Eve (page 94), Christmas Pudding (page 92), Christening Cake (page 64), Lingerie Box (page 52), Bowl of Cherries (page 46).

RICH FRUIT CAKE

This cake is suitable for a Christmas, wedding, special birthday or formal celebration cake. It is moist and fruity and gets better with keeping, so do try to make it well ahead of time. For the larger cakes on the chart it might be easier to make up the mixture the day before, as they need long slow cooking. The mixture can be left overnight in the cake tin(s), covered with a sheet of paper; leave in a cool place until needed.

1 Set the oven to 150°C (300°F) Gas 2. Grease and line the tin(s) (see Lining Tins, pages 15–16).

2 Place the sugar and butter in a warmed mixing bowl and cream until very light and fluffy. This can be quite hard work, especially if it is a very large cake, but it is vital to cream the mixture well to provide a structure for the rest of the ingredients.

3 Add the eggs in small batches, beating well between each addition. Add 5 ml (1 tsp) flour if the mixture begins to curdle. Sift in the flour and spices, then sprinkle in the dried fruit and peel. Fold the mixture together – use your hands for this if you have lots of mixture, it is much easier.

4 Add the cherries, nuts, treacle and rum or brandy. Mix well, making sure all the fruit is combined and there are no patches of flour in the mixture.

5 Turn the mixture into the prepared tin and make a hollow in the centre, to prevent the cake from peaking when it rises. Stand the tin on a double sheet of newspaper or brown paper. Bake for 1 hour at 150°C (300°F) Gas 2, then turn down to 140°C (275°F) Gas 1 for the remaining time.

6 To test the cake, place a warmed skewer into the centre. If it comes out clean, the cake is cooked; if any sticky mixture adheres to it, cook the cake a little longer.

When cooked, leave the cake in the tin to cool. Turn out, leaving it in the greaseproof paper. Prick the top with a fine skewer and paint brandy or rum

RICH FRUIT CAKE ● INGREDIENT QUANTITIES							
Container							
Round tin	*15 cm (6 in)*	*18 cm (7 in)*	*20 cm (8 in)*	*23 cm (9 in)*	*25 cm (10 in)*	*28 cm (11 in)*	*30 cm (12 in)*
Square tin	*12 cm (5 in)*	*15 cm (6 in)*	*18 cm (7 in)*	*20 cm (8 in)*	*23 cm (9 in)*	*25 cm (10 in)*	*28 cm (11 in)*
Pudding basin		*1 ltr (1¾ pt)*					
Fruit tin	*800 g (2 lb)*						
INGREDIENTS							
Brown sugar	150 g (5 oz)	175 g (6 oz)	275 g (10 oz)	350 g (12 oz)	500 g (1 lb 2 oz)	600 g (1 lb 5 oz)	800 g (1¾ lb)
Butter	150 g (5 oz)	175 g (6 oz)	275 g (10 oz)	350 g (12 oz)	500 g (1 lb 2 oz)	600 g (1 lb 5 oz)	800 g (1¾ lb)
Eggs	2–2½	3	5	6	9	11	14
Flour	175 g (6 oz)	225 g (8 oz)	350 g (12 oz)	450 g (1 lb)	600 g (1 lb 5 oz)	675 g (1½ lb)	800 g (1¾ lb)
Mixed spice	1.25 ml (¼ tsp)	2.5 ml (½ tsp)	5 ml (1 tsp)	5 ml (1 tsp)	7.5 ml (1½ tsp)	10 ml (2 tsp)	12.5 ml (2½ tsp)
Currants	200 g (7 oz)	275 g (10 oz)	400 g (14 oz)	450 g (1 lb)	550 g (1¼ lb)	675 g (1½ lb)	1 kg (2 lb 5 oz)
Sultanas	200 g (7 oz)	275 g (10 oz)	400 g (14 oz)	450 g (1 lb)	550 g (1¼ lb)	675 g (1½ lb)	1 kg (2 lb 5 oz)
Raisins	50 g (2 oz)	75 g (3 oz)	100 g (4 oz)	225 g (8 oz)	275 g (10 oz)	350 g (12 oz)	400 g (14 oz)
Candied peel	50 g (2 oz)	75 g (3 oz)	100 g (4 oz)	175 g (6 oz)	225 g (8 oz)	250 g (9 oz)	275 g (10 oz)
Glacé cherries	25 g (1 oz)	50 g (2 oz)	50 g (2 oz)	75 g (3 oz)	100 g (4 oz)	175 g (6 oz)	225 g (8 oz)
Flaked almonds	25 g (1 oz)	50 g (2 oz)	50 g (2 oz)	100 g (4 oz)	100 g (4 oz)	175 g (6 oz)	225 g (8 oz)
Dark treacle	15 ml (1 tbsp)	15 ml (1 tbsp)	22.5 ml (1½ tbsp)	30 ml (2 tbsp)	45 ml (3 tbsp)	50 ml (3½ tbsp)	60 ml (4 tbsp)
Rum or brandy	15 ml (1 tbsp)	15 ml (1 tbsp)	22.5 ml (1½ tbsp)	30 ml (2 tbsp)	35 ml (2½ tbsp)	45 ml (3 tbsp)	50 ml (3½ tbsp)
COOKING TIME	2½ hours	3 hours	5 hours	5–6 hours	6–7 hours	7½ hours	7–8 hours

over the cold cake. (Repeat this process two or three times during storage for a really rich cake.)

STORING
Overwrap the cake and wrappings in sheets of greaseproof paper and tape tightly and neatly. Overwrap the greaseproof paper with doubled foil and tape tightly to make airtight. Place on a really level surface, or a baking sheet, and store the cake in a cool dry place for 2–3 months.

FREEZING
Rich fruit cakes improve with freezing as the process tends to blend and mellow the flavours more quickly. Apart from freezing cut pieces, this is the only real reason for freezing as rich fruit cakes will keep well in tins for a number of years.

Freeze the cakes wrapped as above. Leave plenty of time for thawing, especially for the larger cakes.

LIGHT APPLE FRUIT CAKE

A lighter alternative to the rich fruit cake. Where the fun cake recipes specify fruit cake, use either of these recipes.

1 Set the oven to 180°C (350°F) Gas 4. Grease and line the chosen tin. Sift the flour, bicarbonate of soda and mixed spice into a bowl.

2 Cream the butter or margarine with the sugar until very light, fluffy and pale in colour. Beat in the eggs one at a time, with a spoonful of the flour mixture, then fold in the remaining flour.

3 Mix the dried fruits and peel together and add to the mixture. Peel, core and coarsely grate the apples and add to the mixture together with the marmalade. Stir through evenly.

4 Turn the mixture into the prepared tin, level the top and bake the cake in the centre of the oven for the time suggested in the chart.

To test if the cake is done, insert a skewer into the centre – it should come out clean. If it's ready, remove from the oven and leave to cool in the tin for 5 minutes. Turn out onto a wire tray, still in its wrappings, and leave until cold.

STORING
Light fruit cakes do not keep as well as rich fruit cakes. Wrap as instructed for freezing and store in an airtight container for up to one week.

FREEZING
Do not remove the lining paper from around the cake once it has cooled, but wrap straight from the tin securely in foil. This fruit cake will keep well in the freezer for up to 3 months. Thaw at room temperature for 4 hours.

LIGHT APPLE FRUIT CAKE ● INGREDIENT QUANTITIES			
Container	*1 ltr (1¾ pt) pudding basin 800 g (2 lb) fruit tin*	*20 cm (8 in) round tin*	*20 cm (8 in) square tin*
INGREDIENTS			
Plain flour	100 g (4 oz)	225 g (8 oz)	350 g (12 oz)
Bicarbonate of soda	1.25 ml (¼ tsp)	2.5 ml (½ tsp)	5 ml (1 tsp)
Mixed spice	2.5 ml (½ tsp)	2.5 ml (½ tsp)	5 ml (1 tsp)
Butter or margarine	75 g (3 oz)	175 g (6 oz)	250 g (9 oz)
Light soft brown sugar	75 g (3 oz)	175 g (6 oz)	250 g (9 oz)
Eggs	1	2	3
Raisins	75 g (3 oz)	225 g (8 oz)	350 g (12 oz)
Currants	50 g (2 oz)	100 g (4 oz)	175 g (6 oz)
Sultanas	75 g (3 oz)	100 g (4 oz)	175 g (6 oz)
Cut mixed peel	25 g (1 oz)	50 g (2 oz)	75 g (3 oz)
Cooking apple	50 g (2 oz)	175 g (6 oz)	250 g (9 oz)
Fine-cut marmalade	10 ml (2 tsp)	15 ml (1 tbsp)	15 ml (1 tbsp)
COOKING TIME	1¼ hours	1¼–1½ hours	1¾ hours

QUICK MIX SPONGE CAKE

This super-quick cake keeps moist for several days due to the addition of the evaporated milk.

1 Set the oven to 160°C (325°F) Gas 3. Grease and line the cake tin required.

2 Place all the ingredients in a large bowl or food processor and beat or process for 1–2 minutes until completely smooth.

3 Spoon the mixture into the prepared tin. Bake in the centre of the oven for the specified time or until golden and firm to the touch.

Leave to cool in the tin for 2–3 minutes, then turn out on to a wire cooling rack. Peel away the lining papers while the cake is still warm.

STORING
Keep in an airtight container or wrap in foil for a day. Once decorated, it will keep for 3–4 days after baking.

FREEZING
Allow the cake to cool, then wrap in foil and freeze for up to one month. Thaw at room temperature. If using the sponge to make complicated shapes, it will cut more easily if still half frozen.

QUICK MIX SPONGE CAKE ● INGREDIENT QUANTITIES				
Container	*1 ltr (1¾ pt) pudding basin 800 g (2 lb) fruit tin*	*20 cm (8 in) round tin*	*20 cm (8 in) square tin*	*25 cm (10 in) round tin*
INGREDIENTS				
Soft margarine	100 g (4 oz)	225 g (8 oz)	275 g (10 oz)	350 g (12 oz)
Caster sugar	100 g (4 oz)	225 g (8 oz)	275 g (10 oz)	350 g (12 oz)
Eggs, size 3	2	4	5	6
Baking powder	–	5 ml (1 tsp)	5 ml (1 tsp)	10 ml (2 tsp)
Self-raising flour	175 g (6 oz)	275 g (10 oz)	350 g (12 oz)	400 g (14 oz)
Evaporated milk	45 ml (3 tbsp)	60 ml (4 tbsp)	60 ml (4 tbsp)	90 ml (6 tbsp)
Vanilla essence	2.5 ml (½ tsp)	5 ml (1 tsp)	5 ml (1 tsp)	5 ml (1 tsp)
COOKING TIME	45–55 minutes	1¼ hours	1½ hours	1¾ hours

CHOCOLATE CAKE

Chocolate cake is a perennial favourite and this recipe will be sure to please, especially if it's for *A Big Bar of Chocolate*, see page 40, or perhaps *Chocolate Baskets*, see page 66.

1 Preheat the oven to 160°C (325°F) Gas 3. Grease the tin and line with greaseproof paper.

2 Sift the flour, bicarbonate of soda, baking powder and cocoa into a mixing bowl, then stir in the sugar.

3 Put the butter and milk into a small saucepan and place over a very gentle heat until the butter has melted. Cool.

4 Add the syrup, eggs, melted butter and milk to the bowl of dry ingredients and beat the mixture to a smooth batter with a wooden spoon.

5 Pour the mixture into the prepared tin. Bake for the approximate time shown on the chart, until the cake is firm to the touch and a skewer inserted into the centre comes out clean.

STORING/FREEZING
Allow the cake to cool, then wrap in foil and freeze for up to one month. Thaw at room temperature. If using the cake to make complicated shapes, it will cut more easily if it is still half frozen.

Container	1 ltr (1¾ pt) pudding basin	20 cm (8 in) round tin	20 cm (8 in) square tin	25 cm (10 in) round tin
CHOCOLATE CAKE • INGREDIENT QUANTITIES				
INGREDIENTS				
Plain flour	175 g (6 oz)	275 g (10 oz)	350 g (12 oz)	450 g (1 lb)
Bicarbonate of soda	2.5 ml (½ tsp)	5 ml (1 tsp)	5 ml (1 tsp)	7.5 ml (1½ tsp)
Baking powder	5 ml (1 tsp)	7.5 ml (1½ tsp)	10 ml (2 tsp)	15 ml (1 tbsp)
Cocoa powder, sifted	45 ml (3 tbsp)	60 ml (4 tbsp)	75 ml (5 tbsp)	90 ml (6 tbsp)
Soft brown sugar	115 g (4 oz)	175 g (6 oz)	200 g (7 oz)	275 g (10 oz)
Butter	50 g (2 oz)	115 g (4 oz)	150 g (5 oz)	200 g (7 oz)
Milk	150 ml (¼ pt)	200 ml (7 fl oz)	275 ml (9 fl oz)	325 ml (11 fl oz)
Golden syrup	22.5 ml (1½ tbsp)	30 ml (2 tbsp)	45 ml (3 tbsp)	60 ml (4 tbsp)
Eggs	1	2	3	4
COOKING TIME	45–50 minutes	50–60 minutes	50–60 minutes	1 hour

Most of the recipes in this book only call for a small amount of royal icing to be used. If you have any over from the amount below, then store in a small lidded container in the refrigerator, as it will keep well if kept airtight.

INGREDIENTS

MAKES 225 G (8 OZ)
1 egg white from a size 3 egg
225 g (8 oz) icing sugar, sifted
few drops of glycerine

ROYAL ICING

1 Put the egg white in a completely dry, clean, grease-free mixing bowl and beat it with a fork to break up the white.

2 Gradually beat in the sifted icing sugar with the glycerine to the egg white until the mixture becomes very white and smooth. If using an electric beater, beat for 5 minutes set at the slowest speed.

3 Run a palette knife through the mixture – it should leave a clean mark and the mixture should form soft peaks.

4 If using for piping purposes, leave the icing to stand to disperse any air bubbles that may have formed, which will cause breaks in the piping.

STORING
Keep in an airtight container in the refrigerator for up to two weeks.

This recipe is used for many of the cakes featured in this book, both as a cake coating and a filling.

INGREDIENTS

MAKES 225 G (8 OZ)
100 g (4 oz) softened butter
or margarine
225 g (8 oz) icing sugar, sifted
30 ml (2 tbsp) milk or fruit juice
few drops of vanilla essence or
other flavouring (see below)

1 Place the butter or margarine in a bowl or a food processor and beat or process until soft.

BUTTERCREAM ICING

2 Add the icing sugar, a little at a time, with enough milk to give a spreading consistency. Add flavourings and colourings.

STORING/FREEZING
Store in a lidded container in the refrigerator or until needed. Alternatively, freeze in a plastic bag or container for up to three months.

VARIATIONS
Chocolate Add 40 g (1½ oz) melted and cooled plain chocolate to the icing, or dissolve 30 ml (2 tbsp) cocoa powder

in 15 ml (1 tbsp) boiling water, cool and beat into the icing.
Orange or lemon Omit the vanilla essence and milk and replace with orange or lemon juice and 15 ml (1 tbsp) finely grated rind.
Coffee Omit the vanilla and replace with 15 ml (1 tbsp) strong black coffee, or beat in 10 ml (2 tsp) coffee powder with the icing sugar.
Boozy Omit the vanilla essence and milk or fruit juice and replace with brandy, dark rum or sherry.

Fondant can be made at home or bought from some supermarkets or specialist cake decorating shops. The homemade variety contains liquid glucose, which is available in tubs from chemist's shops.

INGREDIENTS

MAKES 675 G (1½ LB)

675 g (1½ lb) icing sugar, sifted
2 whites from size 3 eggs
30 ml (2 tbsp) liquid glucose
5 ml (1 tsp) glycerine
few drops rosewater (optional)

FONDANT ICING

1 Sift the icing sugar into a large, grease-free, dry bowl and make a well in the centre. Add the remaining ingredients into the well and gradually blend into the sugar with the fingertips.

2 Knead together until smooth, then roll up the paste into a ball and keep in a thick polythene bag until needed. The paste should be smooth and easy to roll. If sticky, knead in a little more sugar until manageable.

STORING
Keep the icing rolled in a ball, tightly wrapped in an airtight polythene bag. It can then be kept in a cool place for up to a week, after which it will start to harden and become crusty.

FREEZING
Not suitable. Fondant icing and fondant-covered cakes become limp and sticky on thawing.

QUANTITY GUIDE FOR COVERING THE TOP AND SIDES OF A CAKE WITH FONDANT ICING

Round cake	Square cake	Fondant icing
15 cm (6 in)	12.5 cm (5 in)	350 g (12 oz)
18 cm (7 in)	15 cm (6 in)	450 g (1 lb)
1 ltr (1¾ pt) pudding basin	–	550 g (1¼ lb)
20 cm (8 in)	18 cm (7 in)	675 g (1½ lb)
23 cm (9 in)	20 cm (8 in)	800 g (1¾ lb)
25 cm (10 in)	23 cm (9 in)	900 g (2 lb)
28 cm (11 in)	25 cm (10 in)	1 kg (2¼ lb)
30 cm (12 in)	28 cm (11 in)	1.15 kg (2½ lb)
33 cm (13 in)	30 cm (12 in)	1.4 kg (3 lb)
35 cm (14 in)	33 cm (13 in)	1.6 kg (3½ lb)

As it is very elastic in texture, sugarpaste is used in tiny quantities to make delicate flowers and models, or it can be mixed with ordinary fondant to make it stronger for looped decorations, etc, producing finer results.

INGREDIENTS

MAKES 450 G (1 LB)

25 ml (5 tsp) cold water
10 ml (2 tsp) powdered gelatine
450 g (1 lb) icing sugar
15 ml (3 tsp) gum tragacanth
10 ml (2 tsp) liquid glucose
20 ml (4 tsp) white vegetable fat
1 egg white from size 2 egg

SUGARPASTE

1 Preheat the oven to 100°C (225°F) Gas ¼. Place the water in a heatproof bowl, sprinkle the gelatine over and leave until spongy. When spongy, dissolve the gelatine in the bowl placed over a pan of hot water.

2 Sift the icing sugar into a separate heatproof bowl and sprinkle the gum tragacanth over the top. Place in the oven for 30 minutes.

3 Place the liquid glucose in a heatproof bowl and gently heat over a pan of hot water, then add to the gelatine mixture

together with the white vegetable fat and stir until blended.

4 Warm the bowl and beater of a heavy-duty electric mixer. Pour in the gelatine mixture, then slowly beat in the icing sugar and egg white until combined. Continue to beat until the mixture is white and stringy.

STORING/FREEZING
Place in a thick polythene bag and keep airtight. Store for 24 hours before use. Use within 1 month, otherwise the paste will start to harden, or freeze in small batches in airtight bags or boxes for up to 6 months.

APRICOT GLAZE

It is useful to have a jar of ready-sieved apricot jam around to save time. Use apricot glaze before covering a cake with almond paste or fondant, or for sticking difficult shapes together. There is no need to cover cakes with apricot glaze before applying buttercream.

INGREDIENTS
MAKES 225 G (8 OZ)
225 g (8 oz) jar apricot jam
30 ml (2 tbsp) water or lemon juice

1 Put the jam and water or lemon juice in a small saucepan and heat gently until the jam has melted. Boil the jam for one minute then pour the mixture through a metal sieve.

2 When cool, pour the sieved liquid glaze back into the jar and discard the pulpy pieces of fruit.

STORING
Keep the glaze refrigerated for up to a month. Always reboil it before use, and apply with a pastry brush.

ALMOND PASTE

INGREDIENTS
MAKES 450 G (1 LB)
100 g (4 oz) caster sugar
100 g (4 oz) icing sugar, sifted
225 g (8 oz) ground almonds
5 ml (1 tsp) lemon juice
few drops almond essence
1 egg or 2 egg yolks, beaten

Use this recipe to cover any of the fruit cake-based recipes in the book.

1 Combine the sugars and ground almonds in a bowl and make a well in the centre.

2 Add the lemon juice, almond essence and enough egg or egg yolks to mix to a firm but manageable dough.

3 Turn on to a lightly sugared surface and knead until smooth. Take care not to overknead or the marzipan may begin to turn oily.

STORING
Wrap securely in polythene or foil and store for up to 2 days before use.

FREEZING
Not suitable.

QUANTITY GUIDE FOR COVERING A CAKE WITH ALMOND PASTE

Square cake	Round cake	Pudding basin	Fruit tin	Almond paste
—	15 cm (6 in)	1 ltr (1¾ pt)	—	350 g (12 oz)
15 cm (6 in)	18 cm (7 in)	—	800 g (2 lb)	450 g (1 lb)
18 cm (7 in)	20 cm (8 in)	—	—	550 g (1¼ lb)
20 cm (8 in)	23 cm (9 in)	—	—	800 g (1¾ lb)
23 cm (9 in)	25 cm (10 in)	—	—	900 g (2 lb)
25 cm (10 in)	28 cm (11 in)	—	—	1 kg (2¼ lb)
28 cm (11 in)	30 cm (12 in)	—	—	1.15 kg (2½ lb)
30 cm (12 in)	—	—	—	1.4 kg (3 lb)

CHOCOLATE ICING

INGREDIENTS
MAKES 225 G (8 OZ)
225 g (8 oz) good quality chocolate, broken into squares
60 ml (4 tbsp) liquid glucose, warmed

This recipe is used for *A Big Bar of Chocolate*, see page 40.

1 Melt the chocolate in a bowl standing over warm water or in the microwave.

2 Stir in the liquid glucose, mix well together, then pour into a bowl and leave to cool completely.

3 Knead the icing until smooth, then roll out between two sheets of non-stick or silicone paper to use.

COVERING A CAKE WITH ALMOND PASTE

Use this method for round, square and all types of shaped fruit cakes.

1 Remove all the paper wrappings in which the cake was baked. Place the cake on a flat surface and roll the top with a rolling pin to flatten slightly. If necessary, trim the top level with a knife if the cake has peaked.

2 Brush the sides of the cake with sieved apricot jam. Sprinkle a clean flat surface with icing or caster sugar and knead one-third of the almond paste. Patch any holes or gaps in the cake sides with small scraps of almond paste.

3 Measure a piece of string around the circumference of a round cake or the length of one side of a square. Roll the kneaded paste into a strip long enough to go around the cake (or four equal strips for a square cake) and wide enough to cover the sides, using the string as a guide for size.

Loosely roll the paste up into a coil. Press one end onto the cake side and then unroll the paste around it, pressing it on as you go.

4 Brush the top of the cake with more sieved apricot jam. Knead the remaining two-thirds of the paste into a round or square and roll out to 0.5 cm (¼ in) thickness, the same shape as the top of the cake and the same size plus an overlap of 1 cm (½ in).

Lay on top of the cake, pressing gently and pushing the overlap into the sides to give an even edge to the top.

5 Press the top and side joins together and smooth out with a palette knife. Leave the almond paste to dry out for at least 48 hours in a cool, dry place or ideally for one week if you are planning to use royal icing. This is vital, as the oils from the paste can seep into royal icing if not sufficiently dried out first.

COVERING A CAKE WITH FONDANT ICING

Once covered with fondant, the cake can be decorated straightaway with a royal icing piped border, or piped or fondant decorations, for example. Crimped patterns can be marked on to the cake, but do these immediately, before the fondant dries and is less pliable.

1 Brush an almond paste-covered fruit cake with sherry or boiled water. Brush a sponge cake with sieved apricot jam to provide a base for the fondant.

2 Roll out the fondant icing 0.5 cm (¼ in) thick on a surface lightly dusted with icing sugar. Move the rolled fondant continually to prevent it from sticking. Measure the circumference of the cake and sides and roll the fondant 2.5 cm (1–2 in) larger, to cover the whole cake.

3 Lift the fondant carefully onto the cake, holding it flat with both hands until it is in a central position, covering the whole cake.

Dust your hands with icing sugar and smooth the icing into position. Flute out the bottom edges, but do not pleat them as this will leave a line.

4 Very gently, smooth down in one direction to remove air bubbles under the icing. Press the fondant on, then trim the edges with a sharp knife. Roll any scraps into a ball and keep tightly wrapped in a thick plastic bag.

5 If any air bubbles remain on top of the cake, prick them with a pin and smooth over. Use the flat of your hand (do not wear rings, or these will leave ridges in the icing) or a special icing smoother to flatten and smooth the top, using a circular movement.

APPLYING BUTTERCREAM

Buttercream can be used as a smooth covering for cakes, piped on in patterns, or made into a decorative design, using an icing comb or the tines of a fork.

● For a smooth finish on the flat area of a cake, spread the buttercream on with a palette knife. Dip the palette knife into a jug of hot water regularly, and keep on spreading the icing and smoothing it out with flat, sweeping movements.

A long icing ruler can also be used to smooth buttercream. Draw the ruler back and forth across the covered area, until the icing is perfectly flat.

● Fill piping bags with buttercream and pipe in exactly the same way you would for royal icing, but using less pressure than for royal icing.

● Buttercream can be coloured with both liquid and paste food colourings. Use natural flavourings like fresh lemon or orange juice for a refreshing lift.

● Buttercream-covered cakes can be frozen for about 3 months, but make sure that there are no dark contrasting colours or sweets that will bleed into lighter colours when defrosting.

CAKE TINS

Cake tins for larger cakes should be made of a good quality metal which holds its shape during the baking process; this is especially important when baking rich fruit cakes. Buy the sizes you are most likely to use regularly, then gradually collect or hire different sized ones as needed. A 20 cm (8 in) round and a 20 cm (8 in) square tin are the most popular sizes and are used for the majority of the cakes devised for this book.

Other containers Cakes can also be baked in a 1 ltr (1¾ pt) ovenproof pudding basin, to give a useful rounded shape for novelty cakes. An 800 g (1¾– 2 lb) tin can that contained fruit or baked beans is ideal for baking small amounts of sponge or fruit cake for the taller-shaped novelty cakes, so save these, carefully washed and dried.

Lining tins For non-stick coated tins, follow the manufacturer's instructions. However, it is advisable to line all cake tins to give cleaner, sharper edges and corners to cakes.

Use oil, melted lard or margarine to grease the tin, then line the tin with non-stick silicone paper or greaseproof paper. Grease the inside surface of the paper, too.

Sponge or chocolate cakes will need one layer of non-stick paper. Light fruit cakes will need 1–2 layers of paper, and rich fruit cakes will need 2–3 layers of paper to protect the sides during the prolonged baking times. As extra protection for rich fruit cakes, tie a double thickness of newspaper or brown paper around the outside of the tin or pudding basin – this prevents the sides from forming a hard crust.

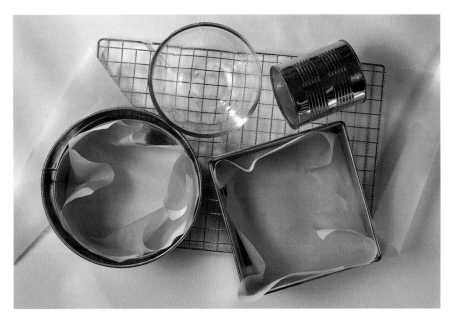

Preparing pudding basins Simply grease the basin well with melted lard or margarine. There is no need to line the basin as the cake will slip out smoothly. Just run a knife around the top of the cooled cake to release it.

Lining fruit tins Grease the top with melted lard or margarine. Line the base and sides with a single layer of greaseproof paper for a sponge or chocolate cake and with a double layer for fruit cakes. Because these tins are rather thin, you may need to wrap a layer of newspaper or brown paper around the outside for fruit cakes.

TO LINE A ROUND TIN

1 Cut a round of greaseproof paper to fit the bottom of the tin. Cut a strip of paper long enough to reach around the outside of the tin with enough to overlap, and wide enough to come 2.5 cm (1 in) above the rim of the tin. Fold the bottom edge up 2 cm (¾ in) and crease it firmly. Open out and make slanting cuts into the folded strip at 2 cm (¾ in) intervals.

2 Grease the tin, and place the strip into the tin to fit the sides, spreading the cut edges over the base. Place the cut out round in the tin over the cut edges.

To double or treble line a tin with greaseproof paper, use the same method as above for each layer of paper.

TO LINE A DEEP SQUARE TIN

Follow the above instructions, but making a square base liner, and making sure that the folds of the long side lining strip go right into the corners.

ICING TUBES

There are many tubes available, varying in size and producing different patterns and designs. They are sold by number, and to increase confusion, not all manufacturers use the same system. However, the plain tubes are all uniformly marked.

To make the novelty cakes described here, you will only need a fairly limited selection, as follows:

PLAIN TUBES: No 0, No 1, No 2, No 3
STAR TUBE: one small and one large
BASKET WEAVE TUBE: medium

When buying tubes, do check that the seams are well joined and that the aperture is evenly shaped. It is worth buying the most expensive models, as

these should last a lifetime. Always clean and dry them thoroughly before storing to prevent rusting.

MAKING A GREASEPROOF PAPER PIPING BAG

Homemade piping bags were used to produce all the piped decorations included here. They are simple to make, so fold several at a time and store them one inside the other.

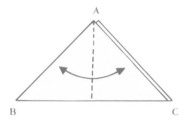

1 Cut a piece of strong, good quality greaseproof paper to a square 25–30 cm (10–12 in) in size and fold in half to form a triangle. Fold the triangle in half again to make a smaller triangle, and open out again.

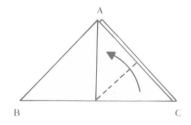

2 Fold point C up to point A and crease firmly.

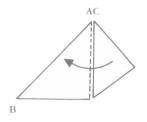

3 Fold the triangle just formed over again along the crease line as marked.

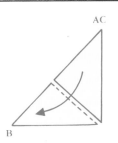

4 Fold point AC down to B and crease firmly . . .

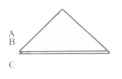

5 . . . to form this shape.

6 Open out to form a cone and fold point BAC over twice and tuck inside the cone to secure. Alternatively, fix with a small staple.

USING A PAPER PIPING BAG

Cut away just enough from the tip to allow an icing tube to fit in securely, then push the tube in place.

Fill the bag no more than half full with icing, then fold the top over twice to completely enclose the icing.

Hold the bag firmly in the palm of your hand and press out just enough icing to make a pattern or a line. Release the pressure on the bag when you want to stop icing.

Don't be tempted to overfill greaseproof paper bags, or they will burst or leak into your hands, or be difficult to hold.

DECORATING EQUIPMENT

Here is a selection of equipment you will find particularly useful for cake decorating. A mini rolling pin is ideal for rolling out small pieces of fondant thinly, and cocktail sticks are vital for making fondant frills. Keep a selection of brushes just for cake decorating as they may get tainted with cooking odours otherwise. A pastry wheel is a good aid for cutting out curved-shaped pieces of fondant. Finally, a small selection of piping tubes and cutters is all you need to complete your basic decorating equipment.

COVERING CAKE BOARDS

Most cake boards come covered in gold or silver paper, but if this is the wrong type of background for your cake, then you can cover them in paper, fondant, or coloured coconut.

● **Using paper** This is also a good way of recycling a used cake board that might have knife marks across it. Use wrapping paper that is resistant to grease if the cake is to be covered with buttercream. Place the board face downwards on a sheet of wrapping paper, and bring the sides up and over the board. Stick the paper to the board with sellotape, keeping it taut. Trim any difficult corners, then overlap them neatly to finish.

● **Using fondant** Lightly brush the board with a little apricot glaze, then roll out fondant thinly. Place over the top of the board and roll flat. Trim away the edges neatly. Use crimpers to make a neat decorative edge, if wished.

● **Using coconut** Spread a little royal icing all over the board, then sprinkle over coloured desiccated coconut. Tap the board to remove excess coconut and leave to dry out for a few hours.

FOOD COLOURING

Always use food colourings in paste form for the recipes in this book. Liquid food colouring will cause fondant to become limp and the icing will not have a good sheen. Paste food colouring will last for a very long time, since you will only need a little at a time. If the colour you require is not available, then blend two basic colours together. For example, for lilac blend pale pink and blue.

Use paste food colouring to colour fondant, buttercream, royal icing and coconut. To use, add a tiny amount with a wooden toothpick and either beat or knead into the icing. To colour coconut, place in a plastic food bag with the colour and rub the bag between the palms of your hands to blend in the colouring.

FRESH WAYS WITH FLOWERS

■ ● ▲

*F*lowers transform a cake, and used in even the most simplest of
decorative ideas can have the most enchanting effect. As well
as using fresh blooms, you can crystallize or sugar flowers to make a
stunning decoration for a cake. Choose the prettiest and most perfectly-
formed flowers you can find, either whole or as petals. Some flowers are
edible, too, which is even better — but make it clear to the recipients
of the cake whether they are or not!

A combination of fresh and crystallized
flowers has been used in this cake
decoration, transforming a simple ring
cake into a stunning centrepiece. Cover
the cake with whipped double cream, as
here, or a creamy-white buttercream,
swirling it up into a spiral pattern with a
palette knife. Arrange a bunch of fresh
roses in the centre of the ring, then
scatter over some sugared rose petals in
varying sizes.

CRYSTALLIZED FLOWERS

Pick or buy the flowers when they are
dry, and try to ensure that they have not
been sprayed with insecticide. Use
blossoms that are just open, and
carefully remove any large green parts.

1 egg white
50 g (2 oz) caster sugar
edible flowers: rose petals, violets,
nasturtiums, primroses

1 Beat the egg white in a bowl with a
fork until just frothy, then use to paint
each flower carefully, using a small
paint brush.

2 Sprinkle each flower with caster
sugar, shaking the sugar over every part
of the petals with a spoon.

3 Place the sugared flowers on kitchen
paper on a wire rack to dry. Leave until
completely dried and crisp before using.
The flowers can be stored in an airtight
tin for up to one day if not using
immediately.

One of the quickest-ever cake
decorations, but also one of the prettiest
– a simple bunch of fresh pink roses and
white gypsophila, tied together with
thin pink ribbon.

This beautiful arrangement of
crystallized flowers sets off an otherwise
plain cake to perfection, making it a
simple but attractive option for a special
occasion or birthday. A variety of
flowers has been chosen, for a
combination of colours and sizes,
together with a few sugared leaves to
balance the composition. Add a pretty
thin silk ribbon in a complementary
shade to finish off, and a lace ribbon
around the base of the cake.

SPECIAL
INTERESTS
■ ● ▲

*W*e have a cake here for every possible interest. *Sporty people will love the cakes for* Anyone for Tennis?, Fore! *and* 30 Not Out!, *and avid gardeners can enjoy their own tiny vegetable patch on* A Bloomin' Good Birthday. *What better to give a seamstress than her own named* Embroidery Sampler, *and the photographer in your family will love to call* Hold It! *with his or her new de luxe camera. Even those poor souls who are forever on diets have not been left out, although our version of a* Slimmer's Lunch for One *is not exactly low in calories.*

A BLOOMIN' GOOD BIRTHDAY

1 Brush the cake all over with apricot jam and place on a 25 cm (10 in) square cake board. If using a fruit cake, cover with almond paste, then leave to dry out for 48 hours.

Colour 800 g (1¾ lb) fondant dark brown. Roll out thinly and drape over the cake. Smooth down with the palms of the hands. Trim away excess edges and smooth down again.

2 Colour 50 g (2 oz) royal icing dark brown and place in a small greaseproof paper icing bag with a large plain tube. Pipe three evenly-spaced horizontal lines round the sides of the cake.

Cut the chocolate stick sweets to the depth of the side of the cake and push into the icing lines at 4 cm (1½ in) intervals, for the fence.

3 Colour 50 g (2 oz) coconut green. Brush an area of the top with honey and sprinkle over the coconut for grass.

Here's a lovely show of home-grown produce for the keen gardener. These vegetables really should win a prize, especially as they were so quick and easy to grow.

■ ● ▲

INGREDIENTS

20 cm (8 in) square sponge or fruit cake
60 ml (4 tbsp) apricot jam, sieved
800 g (1¾ lb) almond paste, for fruit cake
generous 1 kg (2¼ lb) fondant icing
brown, green, red, orange and blue paste food colourings
150 g (5 oz) royal icing
chocolate stick sweets
50 g (2 oz) desiccated coconut
15 ml (1 tbsp) clear honey
9 small wooden skewers

4 Colour 15 g (½ oz) fondant green and shape into beans. Cut the skewers to size and arrange on top of the cake for bean poles. Colour 50 g (2 oz) royal icing green and pipe wiggly lines over the bean canes.

Stick the beans to the royal icing on the canes. When dry, colour 25 g (1 oz) royal icing red and pipe on small red dots for bean flowers.

5 To make the cauliflowers, colour 50 g (2 oz) fondant green and leave 50 g (2 oz) white. Shape both the white and green icings into balls the size of hazelnuts. Flatten out the green icing and wrap around the white balls to represent leaves. Prick the white centres with the tip of a star tube, to make florets. Make three cauliflowers and leave to dry out for 2 hours.

6 To make the carrots, colour 25 g (1 oz) fondant orange and 25 g (1 oz) green. Roll out the green fondant thinly and cut out into leaves as shown. Roll up the leaves. Shape the orange fondant into torpedo shapes and make a hole in the top of each with the end of a paint brush. Make ridges around the surface of each carrot with a cocktail stick (toothpick) dipped in a little brown food colouring. Stick the leaves onto the carrots. Make eight carrots and leave them to dry out for 2 hours.

7 Colour 25 g (1 oz) fondant red and shape into tomatoes. Pipe a small green dot in each tomato. Make about twenty and leave to dry out.

   Colour 40 g (1½ oz) fondant brown and shape into about fifteen potatoes of various sizes and leave to dry out.

8 Colour 15 g (½ oz) fondant light blue and, using a small daisy cutter, stamp into tiny flowers. Pipe some remaining green royal icing onto the sides of the cake and attach the flowers.

   Arrange all of the vegetables on top of the cake.

ANYONE FOR TENNIS?

1 Cut out the cakes and position as shown in the drawings.

Brush the oblong cake all over with apricot jam and place on a 30 × 40 cm (12 × 16 in) cake board. Colour 900 g (2 lb) fondant green. Roll out thinly and drape over the cake and the whole board. Smooth down over the top, sides and board, pressing well into the join, then trim neatly. Re-roll the green trimmings into a thin rope and wrap around the base of the cake.

2 Roll 100 g (4 oz) white fondant into two strips 2.5 cm (1 in) wide and lay in an 'L' shape on the cake and board.

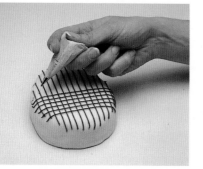

3 To make the racket, colour 100 g (4 oz) fondant cream and roll into an oval. Brush the sponge racket shape with jam and press down the fondant. Fill a piping bag with 50 g (2 oz) royal icing, coloured brown. Snip a small hole in the end of the bag and pipe on lines for the strings.

If you have a friend who spends all of his or her time at the tennis club, a new designer racket makes the perfect present. This one is an exclusive model, and one which is guaranteed to up your friend's popularity rating at the club, too.

■ ● ▲

INGREDIENTS
2 × 20 cm (8 in) square sponge cakes
120 ml (8 tbsp) apricot jam, sieved
1.5 kg (3⅛ lb) fondant icing
green, cream, brown and red paste
food colourings
50 g (2 oz) royal icing

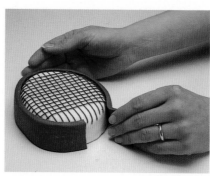

4 Colour 100 g (4 oz) fondant brown and roll into a strip wide enough to wrap around the outside of the racket. Press around the racket, then carefully trim the edges away.

5 To make the handle, re-roll the brown scraps. Colour 75 g (3 oz) fondant red and roll into a 1 cm (½ in) strip. Brush the sponge handle with jam. Cover the handle with brown fondant and wrap the red fondant strip around the bottom half of the handle.

6 Place the two pieces of the racket onto the cake and press to join neatly. Re-roll the red trimmings into three strips. Shape and then position on the sides and base of the racket as shown.

7 To make the tennis ball, shape 50 g (2 oz) white fondant into a round, then mark the ball seams. Place in a metal sieve and roll round gently to give it a fluffy edge. Place the ball on the cake and fix down.

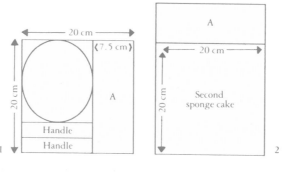

1 The handles measure 12.5 cm × 2.5 cm. Place the handles side by side lengthways on the cake.

2 Add A to the second square to make an oblong.

30 NOT OUT!

1 Brush the cake all over with apricot jam and place on a round 25 cm (10 in) cake board. If using a fruit cake, cover with almond paste, then leave to dry out for 48 hours.

2 Colour 675 g (1½ lb) fondant green. Roll out and drape over the cake. Smooth down the top and sides. Trim away excess edges and smooth down.

Place a card on the cake to keep the wicket plain, then mark around this with a fork to make the grassy pitch.

3 Paint the crease lines on the wicket with white royal icing.

4 Roll 50 g (2 oz) white fondant into a long thin rope and place around the base of the cake to make the boundary.

If you have a cricket-mad man in the family, this cake will bowl him over on his birthday. The only problem is that you will probably be asked to make one for each member of the cricket team, once they've seen it.

■ ● ▲

INGREDIENTS

20 cm (8 in) round sponge or fruit cake
60 ml (4 tbsp) apricot jam, sieved
550 g (1¼ lb) almond paste, for fruit cake
800 g (1¾ lb) fondant icing
green, yellow, brown and red paste food colourings
50 g (2 oz) royal icing

5 To make the bat, colour 25 g (1 oz) fondant yellow-brown, 15 g (½ oz) brown and 15 g (½ oz) red. Make a handle with the brown oblong. Shape the yellow-brown fondant into an oblong bat. Cut a deep 'V' into the bat and trim one end of the handle to fit.

6 Push the handle into the bat and flatten with a rolling pin. Trim away the corners of the bat and round them off.

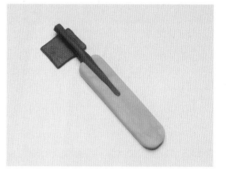

7 Roll the red icing into a strip and wind around the bat handle. Leave the bat to dry for 2 hours.

Roll red and brown scraps into a cricket ball, mark around the centre with a skewer and paint with white royal icing for the stitching.

8 Arrange six cocktail sticks (toothpicks) into two wickets. Roll white scraps into long thin sausages and arrange as a '30'.

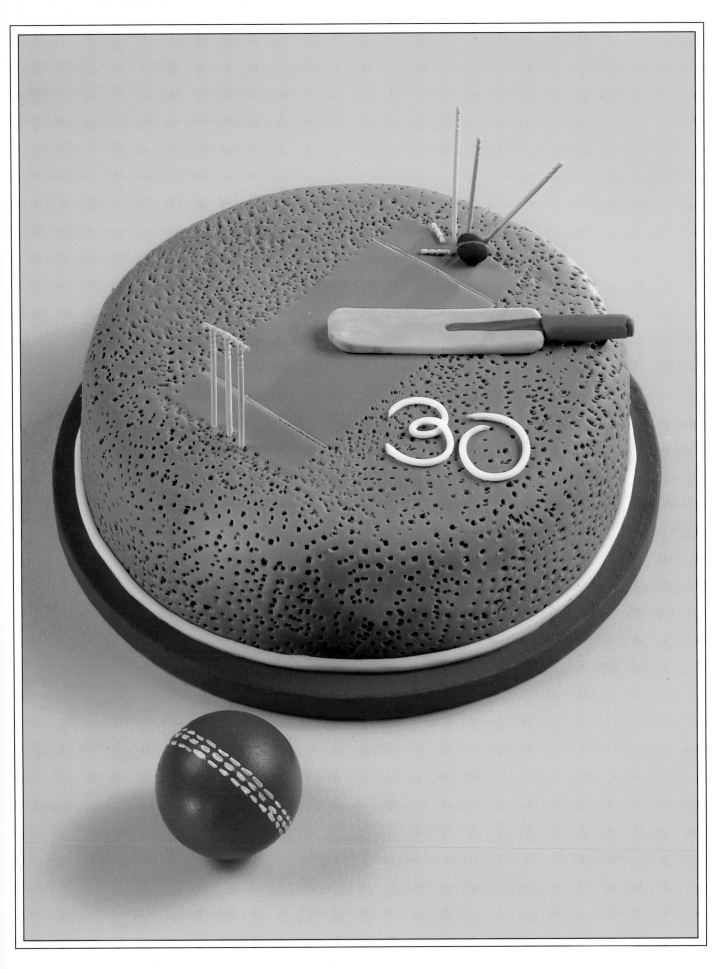

CHOCOLATE DECORATIONS

■ ● ▲

*C*hocolate is the perfect ingredient to create an irresistible decorated

cake in hardly any time. You can spread it over a cake in a smooth

chocolatey coating; you can grate it over a cake for a quick but

effective transformation; or you can create cut-out chocolate leaves and

caraque *for a simple but elegant decoration.*

To make this chocolate-coated cake you will need 100 g (4 oz) plain chocolate, 50 g (2 oz) butter and 4 tablespoons of double cream for a 20 cm (8 inch) cake. Gently heat the ingredients until melted. Cool slightly until the mixture starts to thicken. Pour over the top and sides of the cake.

This tantalizing cake was first coated with chocolate buttercream, spread over roughly with a palette knife. Make chocolate *caraque* as described opposite – about 100 g (4 oz) melted chocolate would be sufficient. Arrange over the top, then sift over a little icing or confectioner's sugar to finish.

Here is a chocolate extravaganza for a special occasion. First coat the cake with chocolate buttercream, then decorate with cut-out chocolate shapes. Arrange a wheel of cut-out triangles, tilted into the buttercream at a slight angle, then press chocolate sticks and cut-out squares around the edge of the cake.

MELTING CHOCOLATE

To melt chocolate for spreading over a cake or for cutting, break it into pieces and heat in a large heatproof bowl placed over a pan of gently simmering water. Stir the chocolate until melted; the bowl should not touch the water, and be careful not to overheat the mixture.

CHOOSING THE RIGHT CHOCOLATE

Choose confectioner's chocolate or eating chocolate if possible. Chocolate-flavoured covering is less expensive and can be used, but the flavour is not as good as real chocolate. Confectioner's chocolate is designed for easy melting, and is good for dipping and coating. Eating, or dessert, chocolate is perfect for spreading and making cut-outs; thin it with a little cream for dipping fruits and candies.

CUTTING CHOCOLATE

1 When you have melted the chocolate, pour it carefully onto a clean, dry flat surface – preferably a marble board. Using a large palette knife, spread the chocolate out quickly, back and forth in a thin layer until just setting. The chocolate will start to turn cloudy when it sets. Leave to cool a little.

2 To make chocolate curls, or *caraque*, pull a long, thin-bladed knife at an angle across the chocolate with a gentle sawing action, scraping off a thin curl. Repeat to make more curls, to the length required. *Caraque* can be stored in a box in a refrigerator until required.

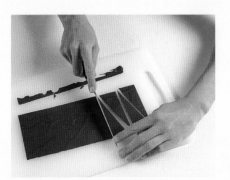

3 To make chocolate shapes, first trim the melted and just-cooled chocolate into a neat rectangle. Cut out triangles with a sharp knife, keeping the edges as straight and neat as possible. Lift the shapes carefully away from the surface using a flat palette knife. Squares and diamonds can be cut by making parallel trellis lines, horizontally and vertically through the chocolate. Cutters can also be used for a variety of other shapes, such as circles, hearts and stars.

CHOCOLATE LEAVES

1 Melt the chocolate in a bowl as described above, then use it to paint the back of a clean and dry leaf (rose leaves are good). Allow the chocolate to dry, then peel the real leaf off very carefully to reveal the perfect chocolate one!

FORE!

1 Using a sharp knife, trim the tops of the two cakes flat. Stick them together with a little apricot jam, then trim them into a round. Brush with apricot jam.

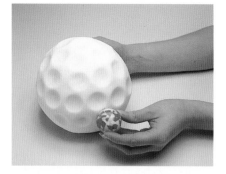

2 Roll out 800 g (1¾ lb) white fondant thinly and completely wrap around the cake. Smooth down all over with the palms of the hands, then make indentations with a ping-pong ball, pressing it at alternate intervals.

This is a must for any keen golfer: a golf ball so big it will be impossible to lose even in the rough. This is one of the quickest and easiest birthday cakes you can make, and it is bound to be a great success at the 19th hole.

■ ● ▲

INGREDIENTS

*2 sponge cakes baked in 1 ltr
(1¾ pint) pudding basins
90 ml (6 tbsp) apricot jam, sieved
900 g (2 lb) fondant icing
ping-pong ball
100 g (4 oz) royal icing
green, red and orange paste
food colourings
50 g (2 oz) desiccated coconut*

4 Colour 75 g (3 oz) fondant reddish-orange. Mould into two torpedo shapes, then flatten out the tops into tee shapes. Dry for 2 hours to harden, in an empty cardboard roll, lined with cling wrap. Place on the cake board.

3 Colour the royal icing green and use 25 g (1 oz) to pipe on 'Happy Birthday' and person's name. Leave to dry out.

Spread the remaining royal icing on a 20 cm (8 in) round cake board. Colour the coconut green, then sprinkle over the board. Place the golf ball onto the wet icing and leave to dry.

EMBROIDERY SAMPLER

1 Place the cake on a 25 cm (10 in) round cake board and secure with a little royal icing. Brush the cake all over with apricot jam.

2 Colour the fondant cream, making a very light tone. Roll out to a round measuring over 35 cm (14 in) in diameter on a surface lightly dusted with icing sugar.

Take a large fluted flan ring and, using the curved edge, roll it round the fondant and cut out a fluted round, 35 cm (14 in) in diameter.

3 Make a dotted pattern around the edge of the fluted round by stamping out small circles with the end of a plain No 2 icing tube.

Do you know someone who is always sewing? This piece of lacy embroidery should keep the keenest seamstress occupied for a few hours on her birthday.

■ ● ▲

INGREDIENTS

20 cm (8 in) round sponge cake
60 ml (4 tbsp) apricot jam, sieved
225 g (8 oz) royal icing
450 g (1 lb) fondant icing
cream, yellow, green, pink, silver and
brown paste food colourings

4 Position the fondant over the cake. Drape the edges to form the fabric, then smooth the top flat.

5 Colour scraps of fondant light brown, roll out and cut out a long strip 1 cm (½ in) wide. Moisten the strip with water, then position around the top of the cake; overlap the ends. Make a small ball into a nail shape and press over the join.

6 Divide up the royal icing and colour a third yellow, a third green and a third pink. Fill a small greaseproof paper piping bag, fitted with a No 1 straight tube, with green icing. Pipe stem and leaf patterns on the cream fondant.

Pipe small pink dots for flowers and to decorate the edge of the 'fabric', with the same tube. Then pipe small yellow flowers and the name of the person chosen. Pipe a raised needle shape at the base and leave to dry. When the icing is dry, lightly paint over the needle shape with silver food colouring.

HOLD IT!

1 Cut the cake into a 12.5 × 20 cm (5 × 8 in) oblong. Cut a 7.5 cm (3 in) diameter round from the remaining piece. Brush the camera body and lens piece with apricot jam.

Colour 675 g (1½ lb) fondant grey. Roll out 450 g (1 lb) thinly. Wrap around the camera body, smooth down and place on a 25 cm (10 in) square cake board. Roll out the remaining 225 g (8 oz) fondant and cover the lens, smoothing down all over.

2 Using a 6 cm (2½ in) cutter, mark a rim around the front of the lens.

3 Colour 450 g (1 lb) fondant black. Roll out 225 g (8 oz) thinly, trim to size and wrap around the camera body. Roll out 75 g (3 oz) thinly, trim to size and wrap around the lens.

Any keen photographer would love an expensive new camera. Here's your chance to give that special person one of the best available for his or her birthday.

■ ● ▲

INGREDIENTS

deep 20 cm (8 in) square sponge cake
60 ml (4 tbsp) apricot jam, sieved
1.15 kg (2½ lb) fondant icing
black paste food colouring

4 Shape buttons, a flash mount and a rewind switch from black and grey trimmings. Leave to dry out on waxed paper for 2 hours before applying to the camera body with a little water.

Paint the words 'Nikon' and 'F2' on the camera body using a small paint brush and black paste colour.

5 Roll grey trimmings into a 0.5 cm (¼ in) thick band and place around the lens. Moisten the back of the lens with a little water and stick the lens to the camera body. Paint on markings and a black rim around the lens.

Roll black trimmings into a strap and drape around the camera.

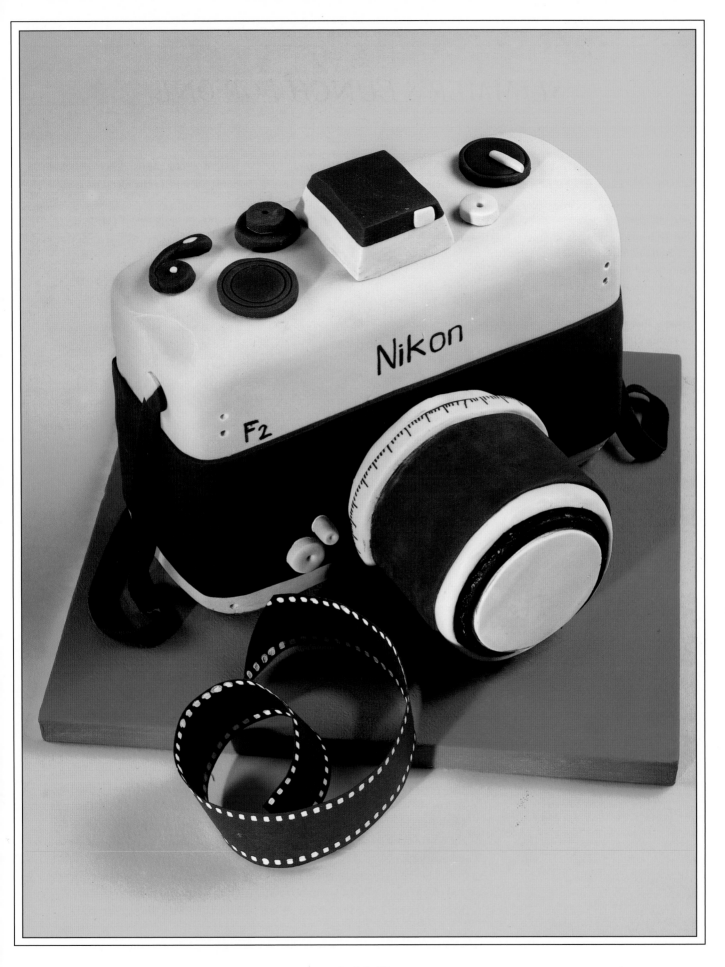

SLIMMER'S LUNCH FOR ONE

1 Brush the cake all over with apricot jam and place on a 25 cm (10 in) cake board. If using a fruit cake, cover with almond paste, then leave it to dry out for 48 hours.

Roll out 550 g (1¼ lb) white fondant thinly and drape over the cake. Smooth down with the palms of the hands. Trim away excess edges and smooth down again. Roll scraps into a ball and store in a strong plastic bag. Wrap the ribbon around the base of the cake.

2 Colour 450 g (1 lb) fondant pale green and roll out thinly. Cut out a 30 cm (12 in) round for a tablecloth, using a fluted flan tin to pattern the edges. Position the tablecloth over the cake, draping the edges to look like fabric.

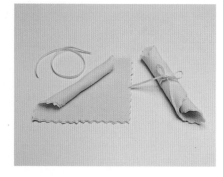

3 Roll 40 g (1½ oz) pale green fondant into a small oblong. Flute the edges with a cocktail stick (toothpick). Roll up the napkin diagonally, then tie up with a ribbon bow.

If you know a weight watcher or belong to a slimming club, this cake is the one to choose. The calories won't help anyone's diet, but the cake itself will cause a few non-fattening birthday laughs.

■ ● ▲

INGREDIENTS

20 cm (8 in) round sponge or fruit cake
60 ml (4 tbsp) apricot jam, sieved
550 g (1¼ lb) almond paste, for fruit cake
1.5 kg (3⅛ lb) fondant icing
very thin peach satin ribbon
green, peach, pink and silver paste food colourings
pink edible-ink marking pen

4 Colour 75 g (3 oz) fondant pale peach pink. Roll out thinly and cut out into a 10 cm (4 in) round. Wrap a plate in cling wrap, smooth over any wrinkles, then press the fondant into the plate. Indent the fondant plate edge with a small star tube, then mark a pink dot in the centre of each star with the edible-ink marking pen.

Colour 50 g (2 oz) pale peach pink and shape fondant into a knife and fork; leave to dry for 2 hours to harden. When

firm, decorate the handles to match the plate, then paint the metal parts with silver colour. Leave to dry out on baking parchment or non-stick paper.

5 To make the lettuce leaf, colour 40 g (1½ oz) fondant green and roll out thinly. Cut out a 10 cm (4 in) round. Flute up the edges by rolling back and forth with a cocktail stick (toothpick). Paint lines on the leaf to resemble veins, using a darker colour green, and leave to dry out for 2 hours.

6 Colour 40 g (1½ oz) fondant very pale peach pink. Cut into a small oblong. Cover a piece of cardboard with cling wrap and fold neatly in half. Drape the fondant over the card and leave to dry out for 2 hours. When dry and hard, write on the lettering in silver.

Remove the plate and card from the cling wrap, and position on the tablecloth with the napkin and leaf.

GIFTS

■ ● ▲

*I*t's such fun to give a friend an unusual and
individual gift for his or her birthday,
especially when you have made it yourself.
The following gifts certainly have a unique quality
about them — the chocoholic will love to receive a
Big Bar of Chocolate, *and fast food maniacs should
be satisfied with a large portion of* Ham 'N' Eggs
or a king-size Birthday Burger. *The* Bunch of
Tulips, Bowl of Cherries *and* Cheers! (*a bottle of
champagne*) *are a little more sophisticated, but the*
Lingerie Box *is guaranteed to raise a smile.*

BIG BAR OF CHOCOLATE

This bar of chocolate should keep even the most ardent of chocoholics satisfied, although it looks as if someone has sampled a bite already.

■ ● ▲

INGREDIENTS

2 × 20 cm (8 in) square chocolate cakes
120 ml (8 tbsp) apricot jam
550 g (1¼ lb) chocolate icing
(see page 13)
gold tissue paper
550 g (1¼ lb) fondant icing
red, cream and brown paste
food colourings

1 Carve squares into one cake, to represent the squares on a bar of chocolate. Trim away one corner of the squared off part, to represent teeth marks, nibbling away a piece of chocolate. Place both cakes together on a large cake board or covered tea tray.

4 Colour 500 g (1⅛ lb) fondant bright red. Roll out the fondant thinly, then drape over the plain area, overlapping the gold tissue paper. Flute the edges of the red icing with your fingers to represent torn paper.

Trim away the edges from the red and chocolate icings. Smooth down the red icing with the palm of your hand.

5 Colour the remaining 50 g (2 oz) fondant cream. Roll out into a wide strip to form a band for the lettering. Place the strip centrally down the red icing, and leave to dry for 2 hours.

Paint the words 'Happy Birthday' on the cream icing in brown food colouring, then paint two thin stripes down each side using a ruler as a guide.

2 Thoroughly brush both cakes all over with apricot jam.

Roll out the chocolate icing thinly, then drape over the squared off part loosely. Press down between the indentations, then smooth over with the palm of the hand.

3 Crumple up the gold tissue paper and place across between the plain part and the squared off part of the cake.

BUNCH OF TULIPS

1 Cut the cake into three as shown and shape the pieces. Stick together with apricot jam and place on a 35 cm (14 in) round cake board. If using a fruit cake, cover with almond paste, then leave to dry out for 48 hours.

Did you forget to buy a birthday or anniversary bouquet? The solution is here, and you'll be surprised how easy these edible tulips are to make.

■ ● ▲

INGREDIENTS

20 cm (8 in) square sponge or fruit cake
90 ml (6 tbsp) apricot jam, sieved
800 g (1¾ lb) almond paste, for fruit cake
1.75 kg (4 lb) fondant icing
pink and green paste food colourings
black edible ink marking pen

4 Roll out 900 g (2 lb) white fondant and use sufficient to cover the cake. Drape over and smooth down. Trim away excess edges and smooth down again. Arrange the tulips and leaves on top of the fondant-covered cake.

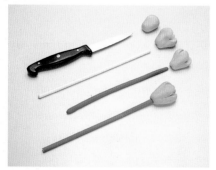

2 To make the tulips, colour 175 g (6 oz) fondant light pink, 275 g (10 oz) dark pink marbled and 450 g (1 lb) green. Divide the light pink fondant into five equal pieces and the darker pink into nine, to make fourteen tulips. For each tulip, shape the pink fondant into an egg shape. Cut off one end square and cut a cross into the other end, then make a hole for the stalk in the square end.

Roll some of the green fondant into short and long stalks, making two at least two-thirds the length of the cake. Fix a stalk into each flower head.

3 To make the leaves, roll out six long, thin sausages of green fondant in varying sizes. Trim away the sides to give leaf shapes. Bend three over cling wrap to shape, and leave to dry.

5 Using thin paper, make a stencil and cut out white fondant to cover and wrap the flowers in.

Use fondant trimmings to make a gift tab and ribbon, and write on the person's name, using the black edible ink marking pen.

BIRTHDAY BURGER

1 To make the lettuce leaves, colour 250 g (9 oz) fondant light green and divide into six 40 g (1½ oz) pieces. Roll each piece out roughly, then roll the edges with a cocktail stick (toothpick) to crinkle. Leave to dry out on crumpled foil for 2 hours.

2 To make the tomato slices, colour 100 g (4 oz) fondant orange-red and roll into a sausage 7.5 × 2.5 cm (3 × 1 in). Cut into six wedges lengthways. Colour 75 g (3 oz) fondant red and cut into 6 sticks 1 × 1 × 7.5 cm (½ × ½ × 3 in).

3 Sandwich the orange sausage back together with the red sticks in between and press together. Colour 100 g (4 oz) fondant red and wrap around the sausage. Cut the sausage into slices. Make pips in the slices with the end of a cocktail stick (toothpick).

This is just the cake to delight a fast-food aficianado – and there's plenty to share round, too.

■ ● ▲

INGREDIENTS

2 × 20 cm (8 in) round sponge cakes
2.3 kg (5⅛ lb) fondant icing
green, red, brown, egg yellow and cream paste food colourings
120 ml (8 tbsp) apricot jam, sieved
100 g (4 oz) royal icing
15 ml (1 tbsp) cocoa powder, sifted
30 ml (2 tbsp) Rice Crispies (Rice Bubbles) cereal

4 To make the paper napkin, roll out 100 g (4 oz) white fondant into a square. Fold the square over and place on a 25 cm (10 in) round cake board. Paint on a decorative border with food colourings.

To make the buns, brush the two sponge cakes all over with apricot jam. Colour 900 g (2 lb) fondant light brown. Roll out thinly and drape 450 g (1 lb) over each cake. Smooth over and neatly tuck the edges underneath. Smooth the fondant down with the palms of your hands.

Colour 550 g (1¼ lb) fondant dark brown and shape into a 20 cm (8 in) round burger.

5 To make the cheese slice, colour 175 g (6 oz) fondant yellow and roll out thinly to a 20 cm (8 in) square.

Place a burger bun on the napkin, arrange three lettuce leaves on this. Place the brown burger on top of the lettuce. Place the cheese slice on top of the burger.

6 Colour the royal icing cream and spoon over the cheese slice to represent mayonnaise. Arrange the tomato slices on top of the mayonnaise, top with the remaining lettuce leaves, then place the other bun in position.

7 Rub a little cocoa powder on top of the bun to colour it. Stick Rice Crispies (Rice Bubbles) on top of the bun with a little royal icing.

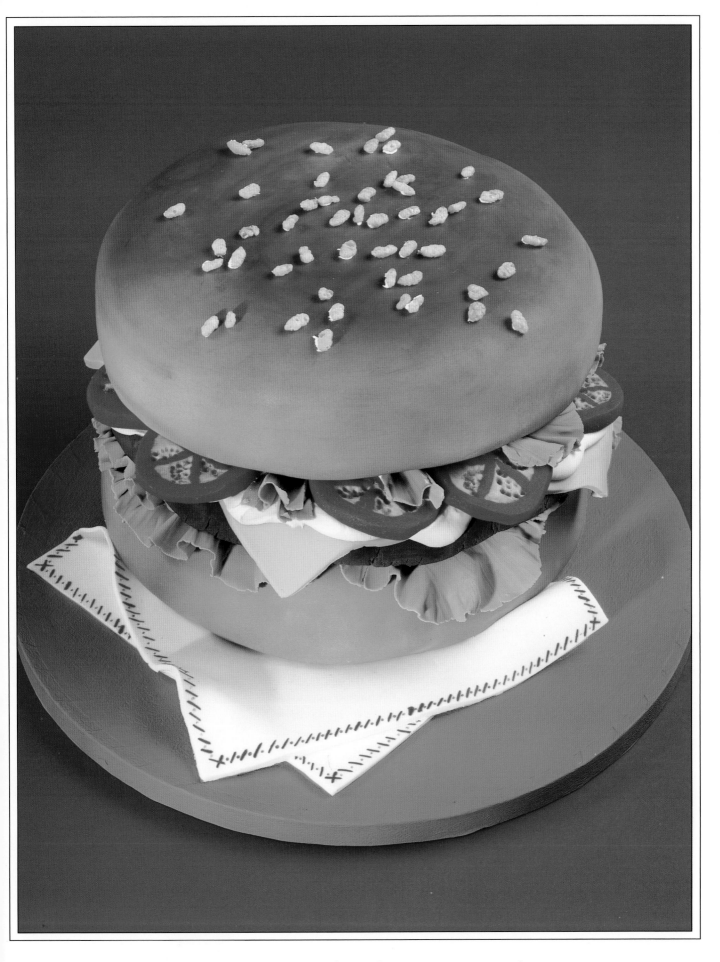

BOWL OF CHERRIES

1 Trim the top of the cake level if it has peaked. Brush it all over with apricot jam and place on a 20 cm (8 in) round cake board.

2 Take 225 g (8 oz) white fondant and roll into long thin sausages. Twist two pieces together, to form a twisted braid.

The perfect cake to bring a smile to anyone's face, however down they may be. The red fondant covers a surprise – real glacé cherries.

■ ● ▲

INGREDIENTS

sponge cake baked in a 1 ltr (1¾ pt)
pudding basin
60 ml (4 tbsp) apricot jam, sieved
900 g (2 lb) fondant icing
green and red paste food colourings
30 glacé cherries
green covered floristry wire
50 g (2 oz) royal icing

3 Starting at the base, loop the braid around the sides of the cake to make the basketwork. Continue looping the twists around the sides until they are completely covered and reach up to the top of the cake.

Colour 225 g (8 oz) fondant green and roll out to a circle large enough to cover the top of the cake. Drape the fondant over the top of the cake, trim to the shape and smooth down. Roll the scraps together and keep in a plastic bag. Press the braiding lightly onto the sides, just covering the green icing.

4 Wash the syrup from the glacé cherries and dry them on kitchen paper. Colour 175 g (6 oz) fondant bright red and roll out thinly. Cover each cherry in a thin layer of fondant, then roll in the palms of your hands to smooth.

Cut floristry wire into short lengths, then loop ends. Place a looped end into each cherry; bend wire to make a stem.

5 Colour the remaining fondant green. Roll out thinly and cut out fourteen green leaves. Mark veins with a sharp knife, pinch the ends together, then press onto the cake. Place the cherries in position and stick to the cake with a little royal icing.

DECORATING WITH RIBBONS AND BOWS

■ ● ▲

If you don't have time to make a proper novelty cake but still want to create something special, why not produce a very attractive cake using just ribbons, rosettes and bows. Very little effort is required to make an otherwise plain cake most appealing, if you select appropriately coloured ribbons and combine them in an effective way. A whole range is at your disposal — thin and thick, serrated or plain-edged, shiny or matt, silk or paper, all in a fantastic array of shades. Secure them to your cake with blobs of royal icing, or pins — but be sure to warn the recipient of the cake if you have used these!

A pretty pastel-blue iced cake is decorated here with the thinnest lengths of pale blue, white, pink and blue ribbon. Double swags around the side of the cake are punctuated with tiny bows, and a single band trims the base. A lovely idea is to place a sprig of fresh, dried or silk flowers on top of the cake, tied with long ribbons of all colours.

This plain white cake has been transformed into a Christmas festive creation with gold, green and red ribbons. A wide red band surmounted with a thinner green ribbon is wrapped around the side, above a contrasting silvery fancy ribbon. A large looped rosette of gold ribbon has two long tails draping over the sides, and is topped with multi-looped bows of thin red and green ribbon, again with swirling trails.

An alternative to real ribbons is to make your own out of coloured fondant. Roll out the fondant and then cut out long strips to the width required – here, tapering strips were cut to give the effect of perspective. Attach four strips to the cake, from the middle of the base of each side up to the centre, securing with blobs of royal icing. A thinner strip, with forks cut at each end, is then looped on top into a bow shape.

HAM 'N' EGGS

1 Brush the cake all over with apricot jam and place on a 25 cm (10 in) round cake board. If using a fruit cake, cover with almond paste, then leave to dry out for 48 hours.

Roll out 450 g (1 lb) white fondant thinly and drape over the cake. Smooth down the sides, trim away excess edges and smooth down again.

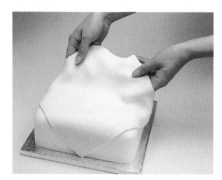

2 Colour 350 g (12 oz) fondant light blue and roll out to a 23 cm (9 in) square. Drape over the cake like a table cloth, fluting the edges out.

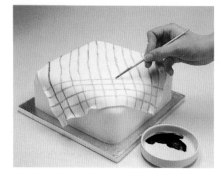

3 Using a paint brush and a fairly strong solution of blue colour and water paint a check pattern on the table cloth.

Some people can eat ham'n'eggs at any time of the day. If it's a favourite meal, serve this cake for a birthday brunch.

■ ● ▲

INGREDIENTS

20 cm (8 in) deep square sponge or fruit cake
60 ml (4 tbsp) apricot jam, sieved
550 g (1¼ lb) almond paste, for fruit cake
1 kg (2¼ lb) fondant icing
blue, yellow, red, grey, orange and brown paste food colourings
cocoa powder

4 To make the plate, colour 50 g (2 oz) fondant yellow and roll out thinly. Cover a 10 cm (4 in) plate or saucer with cling wrap and lay the fondant over the plate. Trim away the fondant edges and leave to dry out for 24 hours until firm.

5 Colour 15 g (½ oz) fondant red and mould into a ketchup bottle. Make a white lid and label from scraps and stick on the bottle. Colour 25 g (1 oz) fondant pale yellow and mould into salt and pepper pots. Colour 25 g (1 oz) fondant grey and mould into a knife and fork. Decorate these items as wished.

6 Shape 25 g (1 oz) white fondant and 7 g (¼ oz) orange fondant to form a fried egg.

Colour 15 g (½ oz) fondant reddish-brown and shape into two bacon rashers. Colour 15 g (½ oz) fondant light brown and shape into three sausages. Dust with cocoa powder, or paint with brown food colouring.

Colour 15 g (½ oz) fondant red and shape into two tomato halves. Leave all the food pieces to dry out for 24 hours, then arrange on the plate. Finally, place the plate on the tablecloth.

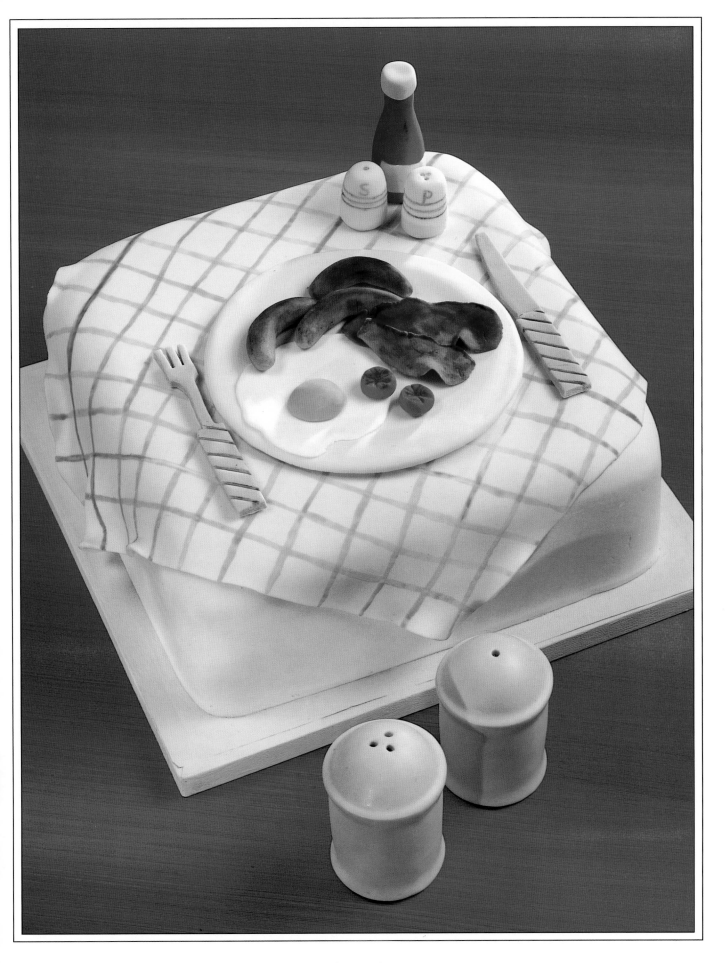

LINGERIE BOX

1 Brush the cake all over with apricot jam and place on a 25 cm (10 in) square cake board. If using a fruit cake, cover with almond paste, then leave to dry out for 48 hours. Colour 550 g (1¼ lb) fondant pink. Roll out thinly and drape over the cake. Flute out the edges to avoid making pleats, then smooth down the top and sides. Trim away excess edges.

While the fondant is still soft, mark sloping stripes into the sides with a ruler.

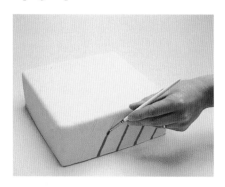

2 Blend a little pink paste colouring with some water and paint in the stripes on the sides.

Make a thin sausage of pink fondant and press around the top edge of the cake to form a ridge.

For a hen party, here is a trousseau offering for the bride-to-be. It's usually accompanied by howls of laughter!

■ ● ▲

INGREDIENTS

20 cm (8 in) square sponge or fruit cake
60 ml (4 tbsp) apricot jam, sieved
800 g (1¾ lb) almond paste, for fruit cake
900 g (2 lb) fondant icing
shocking pink paste food colouring
100 g (4 oz) royal icing
3 white bows
bought sugar flowers

3 Roll out 100 g (4 oz) white fondant thinly to a square large enough to cover the top. Place loosely on top and crumple up to represent tissue paper.

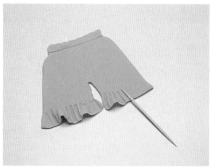

4 Colour the remaining fondant shocking pink. Roll out 100 g (4 oz) and cut out into the shape of a pair of French knickers. Pinch the top together to form a waistband, then roll a cocktail stick (toothpick) around each leg to flute out into frills. Position on top of the paper.

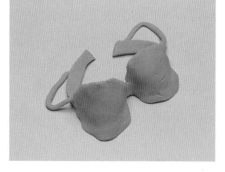

5 Take 75 g (3 oz) shocking pink fondant and shape into a bra with straps. Crimp the edges of the bra, then position on top of the cake.

Fill a small greaseproof paper piping bag with white royal icing and a No 0 tube. Pipe a lacy pattern on the bra and knickers. Position the bows on and stick down with royal icing. Scatter the sugar flowers around the cake and attach with a little royal icing.

CHEERS!

1 Mark the cake into four equal squares and trim each square into a round. Brush each round with apricot jam and stack up, one on top of the other.

Trim down the top two layers to shape like a bottle. Brush all over with apricot jam and cover with thinly rolled almond paste. Dry out for 48 hours.

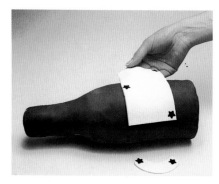

2 Colour 800 g (1¾ lb) fondant dark green. Roll out thinly and cover the bottle, dampening the almond paste with water first. Smooth down over any cracks. Trim away excess edges.

Colour 75 g (3 oz) fondant pale cream and shape into two labels. Moisten the backs and stick in position. Colour 100 g (4 oz) fondant black, cut 25 g (1 oz) out into stars and stick on the labels.

This bottle of bubbly won't go flat once opened, and will make a big impact for any of those special occasions.

■ ● ▲

INGREDIENTS

20 cm (8 in) deep square fruit cake
90 ml (6 tbsp) apricot jam, sieved
450 g (1 lb) almond paste
50 g (2 oz) royal icing
1.15 kg (2½ lb) fondant icing
green, cream, black, brown and red paste
food colourings

3 Colour the royal icing black and pipe onto the labels. Roll out the remaining 75 g (3 oz) black fondant into an oblong 7.5 cm (3 in) deep and long enough to go around the neck of the bottle. Flute out one edge with a cocktail stick (toothpick). Place round the neck, and pull the fluted edge outwards.

Colour a 15 g (½ oz) scrap of fondant light brown and mould into a cork shape. Stick on to the top of the bottle.

4 To make the streamers, colour 75 g (3 oz) fondant red and cut into 1 cm (½ in) strips and wrap around the handle of a wooden spoon covered in waxed paper.

Stand the bottle on a 20 cm (8 in) round cake board. Make a 50 g (2 oz) pale cream fondant congratulations card and pipe on the lettering with black royal icing. Position on the board with the red streamers.

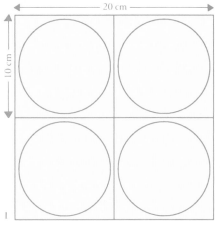

1 Cut the cake into four equal squares. Cut each square into a circle.

20 cm

10 cm

1

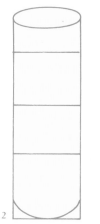

2

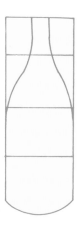

3

2 Stack up the circles.

3 Trim into a bottle shape.

SPECIAL OCCASIONS

■ ● ▲

We hope the ideas in this chapter will help you cater for those slightly more formal occasions when cakes are required as the centrepiece. Our eye-catching wedding cakes, Roses All the Way *and a* Golden Wedding Cake, *have been designed so that they are simple enough for the beginner to attempt. And the* Christening Cake *and* Be My Valentine *cakes are not as complicated as they look; the pretty frills around the base of each cake are particularly easy to achieve. For a retirement party or hen night, we've come up with two really fun cakes –* Happy Days *and* Just Married *– which are guaranteed to liven up any party.*

ROSES ALL THE WAY

1 Brush each cake with apricot jam and place each on a round cake board 5 cm (2 in) larger than the cake. Divide the almond paste in two pieces, one 350 g (12 oz) for the smaller cake and the remainder for the larger cake. Roll out the almond paste and cover each cake, filling in any uneven pieces with paste. Leave to dry out for 48 hours.

Paint each cake with boiled water or the brandy or rum. Divide the white fondant into two pieces, one 350 g (12 oz) for the smaller cake and the remainder for the larger cake. Roll out the white fondant and drape over each cake. Flute out the base like fabric. Smooth down the sides to remove any air bubbles, then flatten out with the palm of your hand or a special icing smoother. Be careful not to pleat the fondant at this stage, or it will leave lines. Trim away the excess at the base, re-roll and store in a strong plastic bag, making sure that no crumbs or jam are in it.

2 To make the twisted border, roll about 225 g (8 oz) pink fondant and about 225 g (8 oz) white fondant into two very long thin sausages. Loosely twist the two sausages together, then carefully place around the base of each cake. Press the join together at the back of each cake. Leave the border to dry out for 24 hours.

This two-tier wedding cake may look complicated, but it was designed for those who are new to cake decorating and doesn't involve any piping work. The trim, side swags and flowers are easy to model from fondant. This also looks delightful as a special one-tier celebration cake.

■ ● ▲

INGREDIENTS

20 cm (8 in) round rich fruit cake
15 cm (6 in) round rich fruit cake
120 ml (8 tbsp) apricot jam, sieved
900 g (2 lb) almond paste
15–30 ml (1–2 tbsp) brandy or rum (optional)
1 kg (2¼ lb) white fondant icing

TRIM, FLOWERS AND ROSES

450 g (1 lb) pink fondant icing
550 g (1¼ lb) white fondant icing
100 g (4 oz) white sugarpaste
yellow paste food colouring
100 g (4 oz) royal icing
4 hollow pillars
4 sticks of wooden dowelling

3 To make the twisted garlands, blend 10 g (4 oz) white sugarpaste into 350 g

(12 oz) white fondant icing. This will make it stronger and more pliable, but it does need to be kept very tightly wrapped and airtight. Roll out the sugarpaste and fondant mixture very thinly into strips 15 cm (6 in) long.

Divide the cake into five sections at the top to attach the loops evenly. Dab the top of the first two sections with a spot of water. Twist one piece of fondant and drape between the two points. Press onto the cake. Continue to loop the twisted strips around the cake, and press them on. Carefully re-roll scraps and keep wrapped.

4 To make the pink roses, colour half the remaining pink fondant a slightly deeper shade of pink. Make a teardrop from the darker shade. Take a small ball of deep pink and flatten out to make a petal shape. Wrap the petal around the teardrop. Make another deep pink petal and wrap this around the first one, pulling the petal edge outwards this time. Using a lighter shade of pink, continue making petals and wrapping them around the rose, pulling out the edges. When the rose is large enough, gently pull away the thick base piece. Mould the base neatly, then leave the rose to dry and harden protected in an egg box lined with crumpled foil. Make ten pink roses in total.

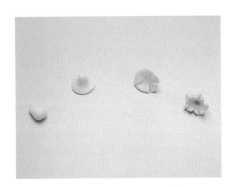

7 Gently mark the positions for the pillars with a skewer. Thread a piece of wooden dowelling into each pillar to take the weight of the cake. This should be deep enough to go right through the cake. Push the skewer right into the fondant; it should be flush with the cake with no wood showing. If it is too long, trim it level. Insert the four pillars at equal spaces.

8 Decorate the spaces underneath the pillars with the remaining roses and white flowers, attached with small dabs of royal icing. Leave to dry out for 24 hours.

Roll out the remaining pink fondant very thinly and, using a daisy cutter, stamp out thirty daisies. Attach at the join to each loop, and scatter around the top and central floral decorations.

5 To make the white flowers, mould a small ball of the white fondant and sugarpaste mixture into a teardrop shape. Flatten out the top edge to form a Mexican hat shape. Snip the hat into five petals with a small pair of nail scissors. Pinch each petal together into a pointed 'V' shape. Mould the centre by using a fluted moulding tool or biro (ball point pen) top. Make twenty-two star flowers. Leave to dry out for 24 hours. When dry, dab a tiny amount of pale yellow colouring into the centre of each.

6 Make the top decoration: make a small ball from white fondant scraps and flatten down into a small mound. Press the mound onto the centre of the top tier. Press six roses and sixteen white flowers into this; make the top higher and fill the side sections to cover the fondant base. Leave to dry for 24 hours.

JUST MARRIED

Make this cake for an eve of
wedding party. Marriage should
be a time of celebration, and the
more fun the better!

■ ● ▲

INGREDIENTS

20 cm (8 in) square sponge or fruit cake
90 ml (6 tbsp) apricot jam, sieved
800 g (1¾ lb) almond paste, for
fruit cake
800 g (1¾ lb) fondant icing
peach, black, red and yellow paste
food colourings
scraps of lace netting
50 g (2 oz) royal icing
white floristry wire

1 Brush the cake all over with apricot
jam and place on a 25 cm (10 in) square
cake board. If using a fruit cake, cover
with almond paste, then leave to dry out
for 48 hours.

Roll out 450 g (1 lb) white fondant
thinly. Place a thin strip around the
lower half of the sides, next to the
board. Take the remaining rolled icing
and loosely drape over the top and sides
of the cake. Make the sheets by tucking
under a fold of fondant at each corner.
Flatten out the top and smooth over
with the palms of your hand.

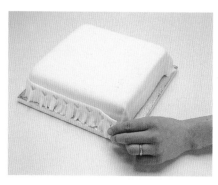

2 To make the base frill, roll out scraps
thinly into four 20 cm (8 in) strips. Cut
a fluted edge with a pastry wheel. Flute
up the edges with a cocktail stick
(toothpick), by rolling backwards and
forwards. Cut out small hearts with a
heart-shaped cutter. Stick each frill strip
onto the cake with boiled water. Neaten
the join with a ruler.

Make the bolster by rolling out a
sausage from 25 g (1 oz) white fondant.
Make two oblong pillows from 50 g (2 oz)
white fondant, then crimp the edges to
form lace. Place pillows on the bolster.

3 Model two heads, four hands and two
large and two small feet from 50 g (2 oz)
flesh-coloured fondant. Make fingers
and toes by snipping with tiny nail
scissors. Paint faces on the heads and
leave to dry.

Roll out 100 g (4 oz) white fondant
thickly to form the bedcover. Roll one
end thinly for the turnover. Crimp the
edges of the cover all around. Place the
heads on the pillows. Make two oblongs
from scraps of fondant for the bodies and
place in the bed next to the heads.

4 Take the bedcover and position over
the bodies. Turn down the top. Stick
hands and feet in position with a little
royal icing. Lightly stamp out hearts on
the bedcover.

Make a hat from grey-coloured scraps
of fondant. Bunch up the lace netting
for the veil and secure with white
floristry wire. Pipe hair onto the bride
and groom. Place the hat and veil in
position. Paint the stamped-out hearts
on the bedcover in red.

Roll out a piece of fondant thinly to a
square and leave to dry out for 2 hours.
Paint on the message 'Just Married'.

GOLDEN WEDDING CAKE

1 Brush the fruit cake all over with apricot jam and place on a 25 cm (10 in) round cake board. Roll out the almond paste, cover the cake and leave to dry out for 48 hours.

Roll out 675 g (1½ lb) white fondant thinly and drape over the cake. Smooth down over the top and sides, fluting out the edges to avoid pleats. Trim away excess edges, then smooth down the sides again.

2 Pin a greaseproof paper template to the sides of the cake, with six loops equally marked on to it. Transfer the loops to the side of the cake by pricking through the paper with a pin.

Colour 75 g (3 oz) royal icing peach and pipe a shell border around the bottom edge of the cake.

3 To make the lacework on the sides, copy the shape drawn opposite onto white card. Place the card under a piece of waxed paper. Fill a greaseproof paper piping bag, fitted with a No 0 or 1 plain tube, with white royal icing. Pipe over the design onto the waxed paper, then leave to dry. Make fifty shapes (which allows for some breakages).

Colour 50 g (2 oz) fondant peach, roll out and stamp out one hundred blossom flowers with a medium-sized blossom cutter. Leave to dry out for 2 hours.

When a couple have been married for fifty years they really deserve a lovely cake to celebrate the occasion. This cake is easier to make than it looks, and can be put together in simple stages.

■ ● ▲

INGREDIENTS
20 cm (8 in) round fruit cake
90 ml (6 tbsp) apricot jam, sieved
550 g (1¼ lb) almond paste
850 g (1⅞ lb) fondant icing
900 g (2 lb) royal icing
peach and green paste food colourings
bright peach stamens
peach dusting powder
waxed paper

4 To make the large flower, colour 75 g (3 oz) fondant peach and mould into six large petals. Frill the edge of each petal by rolling back and forth with a cocktail stick (toothpick). Leave to dry out on crumpled foil.

Assemble the flower by sticking the petals together with royal icing. Pipe royal icing into the centre, then stick the peach stamens into this.

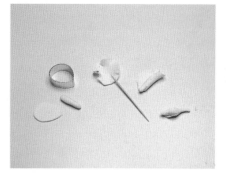

5 To make the buds, mould six more petals in the same way, make six sausage shaped centres and wrap each petal around a sausage. Leave to dry out for 4 hours. Lightly dust the flower and buds with peach dusting powder.

Colour 50 g (2 oz) fondant green and mould into 7–8 leaves. Mark on veins with a sharp knife and leave to dry out for 2 hours.

6 Stick the lacework and stamped out flowers to the loops on the sides with royal icing. Pipe on large peach dots, using a No 2 or 3 plain tube.

Position the flower, buds and leaves on top and stick on with royal icing. Pipe on '50' using a No 2 plain tube and peach royal icing.

Template for lacework

CHRISTENING CAKE

1 Brush the cake all over with apricot jam and place on a 25 cm (10 in) round cake board. Roll out the almond paste, cover the cake and leave to dry out for 48 hours to harden.

To make the rabbit, colour 75 g (3 oz) fondant brown. Shape 25 g (1 oz) into a pyramid for the body and 15 g (½ oz) into a conical shaped head. Mould two ears and leave to dry out. Stick the ears on the head with a little royal icing. Mark on eyes, nose and whiskers.

2 To make the clothes, colour 50 g (2 oz) fondant pink and roll out thinly. Cut out a 6 cm (2½ in) round with a fluted pastry cutter, then cut out the centre and a small wedge. Flute up the edges with a cocktail stick (toothpick). Make a white frill long enough to go around the body from a long narrow strip, fluting the edges in the same way. Make a small white tail from scraps and stick on the body.

This is a delightful cake to make for a baby's Christening party. The rabbit may look tricky, but follow the simple steps for a stunningly successful outcome.

■ ● ▲

INGREDIENTS

20 cm (8 in) round fruit cake
90 ml (6 tbsp) apricot jam, sieved
550 g (1¼ lb) almond paste
900 g (2 lb) fondant icing
green, pink, brown and yellow paste food colourings
100 g (4 oz) royal icing
thin pink satin ribbon

3 Wrap the petticoat around the body, then attach the dress on top. Roll pink fondant scraps into two arms. Make two white cuffs, two brown paws, one white collar and two small white buttons.

4 Attach to the rabbit as shown, and stick the head to the body.

5 To make the daisies, take a small ball of white fondant and make into a torpedo shape. Flatten out one end, then shape the other into a stalk. Using tiny scissors, snip the flattened edges into petals. Prick the centre with a cocktail stick (toothpick). Paint around the edges with a very pale pink colour and colour the centre yellow.

Colour 15 g (½ oz) fondant green and mould green leaves.

6 Brush the almond-paste covered cake lightly with boiled water or a spirit, such as brandy. Roll out 675 g (1½ lb) white fondant and drape over the cake. Smooth down with the palms of your hand. Trim away excess edges, then smooth down again.

7 Using royal icing, pipe a border of small dots around the bottom edge of the cake. Make six looped frills (see page 82, step 2) – brush one side of each fondant strip with pink, then flute the coloured edge. Attach around the cake. Pipe a small line of dots on the edge of the loops; attach a small pink bow on top of each loop.

Place the rabbit on top, and arrange the daisies and leaves. Pipe swirls around the flowers with royal icing. Colour a little royal icing pink or blue, and pipe on the child's name.

CHOCOLATE BASKETS

1 Place the large cake on a 30 cm (12 in) round cake board and trim the top level if it has peaked. If the cake is to be kept for any length of time, sprinkle it with about 45 ml (3 tbsp) of the liqueur or brandy if liked, which will keep it moist.

Take 100 g (4 oz) chocolate buttercream and smooth over the top and sides of the cake with a palette knife. This will give you a good flat surface to pipe onto.

2 To make the basketweave, fill one greaseproof paper piping bag with a No 2 tube and chocolate buttercream, and another with a basketweave tube and more chocolate icing. Beginning at the back of the cake and holding the basket weave tube at an angle, pipe three or more lines about 2.5 cm (1 in) long, one above the other, with the width of the tube left between them. Next, with the plain tube, pipe a straight vertical line down the edge of the horizontal line.

Take the basket tube again and pipe in more lines the same length as the first ones to fill in the gaps, but beginning halfway along those already piped, and covering the straight lines. Pipe another straight vertical line down the side and continue to build up the basketweave around the sides of the cake, taking care to keep it even.

A garland of pretty silk flowers tumble down the sides of this pretty chocolate basketweave celebration cake. The lucky recipient can keep and mount the flowers as a permanent reminder of an extra-special cake.

■ ● ▲

INGREDIENTS

25 cm (10 in) round chocolate cake
20 cm (8 in) round chocolate cake
60 ml (4 tbsp) liqueur or
brandy (optional)
1 kg (2¼ lb) chocolate buttercream icing
bought bunches of silk flowers, in large
and small sizes
thin satin ribbon
floristry wire

When the sides of the cake are completely covered, pipe on a neat border around the top edge.

3 Trim the other cake completely flat and sprinkle with liqueur. Place on top of the other cake and cover with 90 ml (6 tbsp) buttercream. Spread completely flat on top with a palette knife.

Continue to pipe and weave the icing around the sides, as instructed before, and finish off with a border again.

4 Leave the icing to harden slightly for 4 hours, then arrange large and small sprays of silk flowers and leaves, trailing them up one side of the cake. Try not to position the flower heads too close to the actual icing, as the fat in the icing may seep into them.

5 Make loops from satin ribbons, secure with floristry wires, then stick the wire stemmed bunches of ribbon into the cake between the flower sprays.

Serve the cake on the same day of making if possible, or keep for just one day, refrigerated without the flowers and ribbons in position.

HAPPY DAYS

1 Brush the cake all over with apricot jam and place on a 25 cm (10 in) square cake board. Colour 800 g (1¾ lb) fondant cream. Roll out thinly and drape over the cake. Smooth over the top and sides, then flute out the bottom edges, without pleating them. Trim away the excess edges and re-roll the scraps. Smooth down the top and sides with the palms of your hands or with an icing smoother.

Someone retiring at work? Make it a real sendoff with a fun cake to wish a colleague all the very best. No armchair and slippers here; streamers and poppers set the scene for a celebration.

■ ● ▲

INGREDIENTS

20 cm (8 in) square sponge or chocolate cake
60 ml (4 tbsp) apricot jam, sieved
1.2 kg (2¾ lb) fondant icing
cream, pink, turquoise blue, red and yellow paste food colourings
feather
string
colourful ribbon for base of cake

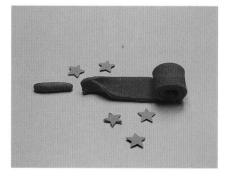

4 Use 25 g (1 oz) red fondant to make a party trumpet. Shape the red fondant into a long thin strip, then roll up loosely. Leave to dry for 2 hours. Stamp out a few stars from a little fondant, and stick on the curled end. Make the mouthpiece from scraps of yellow fondant, about 25 g (1 oz), and stick to the front. Stick the feather on one side and attach the trumpet to the cake.

2 Divide the remaining scraps and enough fondant to make three 100 g (4 oz) pieces. Colour one piece dark pink, one piece turquoise blue and the remaining piece yellow. Roll out 100 g (4 oz) of each colour very thinly.

3 Cut into long thin strips for the streamers. Drape the streamers loosely over the top of the cake, looping and twisting them in a haphazard way.

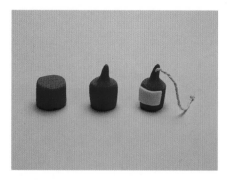

5 Make party poppers from 15 g (½ oz) scraps of fondant and some red fondant. Roll into sausage shapes, chop into pieces, then pinch one end into a long stem and attach a short piece of string. Make a label from scraps and stick to the front. Paint 'Party Poppas' on the label with food colouring.

Roll out 25 g (1 oz) white fondant into a thin white oblong. Trim the edges and paint on the words 'Happy Days'. Leave to dry for 2 hours, then stick onto the cake.

BLUE SUEDE SHOES

If you can remember the Fifties, there's only one way to cope with a fortieth birthday – rock 'n' roll the night away with a pair of blue suede shoes.

■ ● ▲

INGREDIENTS
20 cm (8 in) square chocolate sponge or fruit cake
90 ml (6 tbsp) apricot jam, sieved
800 g (1¾ lb) almond paste, for fruit cake
1.15 kg (2½ lb) fondant icing blue, orange and black paste food colourings

1 Cut the cake in half down the middle. Trim the front end of each half into a point, then cut a curve into the middle on each side. Round-off the back to make the shape of a winklepicker shoe. Keep the cut scraps to one side.

Brush each shoe all over with apricot jam. Take the cut pieces and build up the heel ends of the shoes so that they are higher at this end, then shape down towards the toes. Brush with jam again. If using a fruit cake, cover with almond paste, then leave to dry out for 48 hours.

2 Colour 800 g (1¾ lb) fondant blue and roll out thinly. Drape half over each shoe and press into the corners to mould into a shoe shape. Keep blue scraps and re-roll, being careful not to roll in any crumbs or jam.

3 Colour 100 g (4 oz) fondant orange. Mould into shape and place one on top of each shoe.

Roll out the remaining blue fondant into two squares and cut out shapes for the top of the shoes. Cut out two tongue shapes from the fondant and place over the orange fondant. Mark all along the edge of each tongue with a skewer to represent stitching.

Dampen the top and sides of each shoe and wrap the shoe top around. Press into place and trim if necessary. Prick all along the edges of each shoe top with a skewer to represent stitching.

4 Colour 225 g (8 oz) fondant black. Roll out into a strip 2.5 cm (1 in) wide for each shoe. Dampen the base of each shoe, then wind the black fondant strip around. Press neatly into place, then make ridges into the sides with a knitting needle or skewer to represent crepe rubber soles.

Mark 8 lace holes into each shoe with a skewer. Roll remaining scraps into two long thin sausages and position pieces in lace eyelets. Drape the two top laces loosely. Place the shoes on a 30 cm (12 in) cake board.

Template for blue suede shoe, reproduced one third actual size.

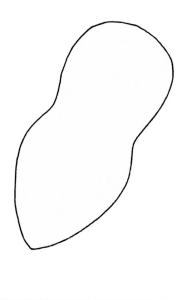

QUICK IDEAS WITH PIPING JELLY

■ ● ▲

Piping jelly or gel, and royal icing, are available commercially pre-prepared in tubes all ready for use. They come in a great range of colours and shades, and are perfect for quick and easy cake decoration, without the need to make up special batches of icing. Use them in the same way as you would a normal icing bag: although of course you won't have the range of tips and tubes at your disposal, clever effects can still be achieved.

This special 21st-birthday cake is decorated in shades of yellow, which with the shiny light grey ribbon created a gold-and-silver effect. A large six-pointed looping star was first piped on, with another just inside it. The areas enclosed by the star around the edge of the cake were filled in with little scrolls and twists of piping, and a zig-zag border was piped around the base. The '21' was piped freehand, but you could follow a pin-pricked outline from a trace guide if you are not confident enough to do this.

PIPING A BORDER

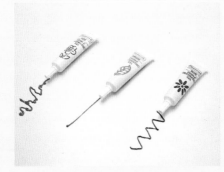

A range of patterns are possible with ready-made piping gel, such as straight lines, looping lines, zig-zags and trelliswork. Practise on a piece of paper until you feel confident enough to pipe directly onto the cake.

This pretty border design starts off with an outline of tiny piped yellow dots. Then, begin to loop them together with a continuous line of icing in a contrasting colour. Work your way gradually around the cake, turning it as you go to make the angle of application easier (if you have a turntable, this will help).

A pink fondant-covered cake is piped over in red, for a strong impact. A continuous looped line has been piped around the top edge of the cake, then a large heart is created with a line of tiny dots. Inside, the birthday message outline was made with an embosser (see page 81) and this was used as a guide to pipe over. A small dotted heart was added below.

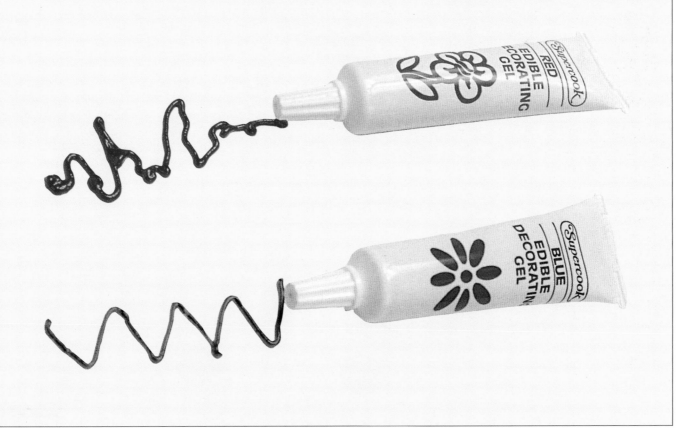

BE A PIG ON YOUR BIRTHDAY

1 Trim the top of the cake flat if it has peaked, and lay upside down on a board. Trim away the peaked top and the front quarter from the other cake and lay it on its side. Trim the cut quarter to form a snout shape. Place the pig on a 30 cm (12 in) cake board.

Over the last few years, pigs seem to have gained in popularity. They already feature on lots of cards and wrapping paper, so why not make a cake to match? If you have a friend who really enjoys food, then this is his or her cake.

■ ● ▲

INGREDIENTS

*2 × sponge cakes baked in 1 ltr (1¾ pt)
pudding basins*
450 g (1 lb) buttercream icing
green and pink paste food colourings
4 pink and 2 white marshmallows
100 g (4 oz) fondant icing
pink and red Smarties (M & Ms)
50 g (2 oz) desiccated coconut

4 Colour the fondant icing pink, then mould into two ears, a tail and two nostrils. Pinch the base of each ear together and place on either side of the head. Twist the tail up and place at the back of the pig. Flatten out the nostrils and place on the snout.

5 Stick a pink Smartie on each eye and a red one below the snout to make the mouth. Place two pink marshmallows at the front and two marshmallows at the centre for trotters.

6 Colour 60 ml (4 tbsp) buttercream green and spread thinly over the cake board. Colour the desiccated coconut green, sprinkle lightly over the cream on the board and press down. Scatter with red and pink Smarties.

2 Colour the buttercream icing a light pink and spread all over the cakes, including the join in between them. Place the snout shape in the middle of the face and spread over with buttercream icing.

Smooth the icing flat with a small palette knife.

3 Place two white marshmallows either side of the snout to make the eyes.

THE DO-IT-YOURSELF CAKE

1 Brush the cake all over with apricot jam. Roll out 675 g (1½ lb) white fondant thinly and drape over the cake. Smooth down over the top and sides with the palms of your hands. Trim away excess edges and smooth down again. Roll up scraps and keep in a strong plastic bag. Place the cake on a 25 cm (10 in) square cake board.

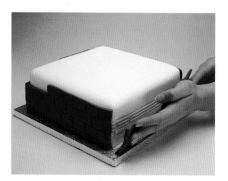

2 Colour 350 g (12 oz) fondant a reddish-brown colour for the bricks and roll out oblongs 20 × 7.5 cm (8 × 3 in). Mark out the brickwork using a sharp knife, then cut out bricks at random. Dampen lightly with water and stick to the sides of the cake. Shape the trimmings into extra oblong bricks for the top and leave to dry out for 2 hours.

3 To make the saw, colour 25 g (1 oz) fondant grey and 25 g (1 oz) brown. Roll out the grey fondant and mark the straight sides of the blade with a knife. Cut out the zig-zag edge of the saw with a pastry wheel.

Roll out the brown fondant and cut out the handle shape. Moisten the join and stick the two pieces together. Leave to dry out on waxed paper for 2 hours until firm.

If you've friends who have just moved into a new home, then this cake should help them through their home improvements. It makes a great finale to a decorating party, too.

■ ● ▲

INGREDIENTS

deep 20 cm (8 in) square sponge cake
60 ml (4 tbsp) apricot jam, sieved
1.5 kg (3⅛ lb) fondant icing
red, brown, black, cream and green paste food colourings
thin white floristry wires

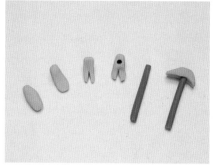

4 To make the hammer, colour 15 g (½ oz) fondant grey and 15 g (½ oz) brown. Make a grey oval, flatten out one end, then cut 0.5 cm (¼ in) into the narrow end. Make a small hole for the handle. Roll the brown fondant into a handle, then fix the handle to the hammer head.

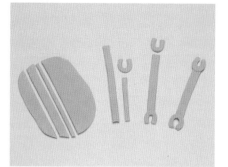

5 To make the spanners, colour 25 g (1 oz) fondant grey, roll out and cut into one thin strip and one medium strip. Cut the thin strip in quarters and bend into four horseshoe shapes. Cut the thicker strip in half and attach the ends to the horseshoe shapes. Leave the spanners to dry out for 2 hours.

6 To make the brushes, colour 50 g (2 oz) fondant cream, then mould into brush shapes. Mark a line across with a knife, then mark on the bristles. Paint the handles brown and leave to dry out for 2 hours.

To make the planks of wood, colour 50 g (2 oz) fondant a light brown marbled colour by kneading the colour into the fondant lightly to give a streaky effect. Cut into strips and leave to dry out for 2 hours.

7 To make the paint pots, roll 75 g (3 oz) white fondant into a short sausage. Cut into three rounds, trim the top and bottom flat, then indent the top. Make handles from thin white floristry wires. Paint the tops and the brushes different colours, then leave to dry out for 2 hours.

Finish by painting the words 'Good Luck' onto the cake, and arranging the pieces on top.

GET WELL SOON

1 Cut a strip 6 cm (2½ in) wide and 20 cm (8 in) long down one side of the cake, and then cut the strip in half. Place the two halves upright side by side at the top of the long slab to make a support for the headboard. Coat all the surfaces with apricot jam and stick them together.

2 Colour 675 g (1½ lb) fondant cream. Roll out 450 g (1 lb) thinly, drape over the sponge cake pieces and press lightly to smooth over. Trim away the excess edges. Place the cake on a 25 cm (10 in) square cake board.

Colour 75 g (3 oz) fondant green. Roll out the position around the cake to make the mat. Crimp the edges and mark a criss cross pattern on the mat with a pastry wheel.

A perfect pick-me-up for a friend who's temporarily confined to bed — a less than agile skier perhaps. It will be sure to speed the patient's recovery.

■ ● ▲

INGREDIENTS

20 cm (8 in) square sponge cake
60 ml (4 tbsp) apricot jam, sieved
900 g (2 lb) fondant icing
cream, green, peach, brown, orange, red, green and blue paste food colourings

3 Colour 50 g (2 oz) fondant flesh-colour. Roll 25 g (1 oz) into a ball for the head. Shape 25 g (1 oz) cream fondant into a pillow and pinch the edges straight.

Colour 75 g (3 oz) fondant mid-brown for the head- and footboard. Roll out thinly and position at the base and head of the bed. Using a sharp knife, cut a curved pattern into the fondant.

4 Place the pillow on the headboard and the head on the pillow. Make an oval body shape and place in the bed.

Make two feet and two arms with the remaining flesh fondant. Roll thin strips of white fondant around one leg and one arm to form a plaster cast on each. Position arms and legs on the bed.

5 Roll out 225 g (8 oz) cream fondant thickly. Flute the edges and turn over the top edge. Drape over the bed to make the coverlet. Paint the coverlet with coloured squares.

Paint a face and hair on the head. Roll scraps of white fondant and colour green, then model into an ice pack and place on top of head. Finally, roll out a piece of white or cream fondant to make a 'Get Well Soon' sign.

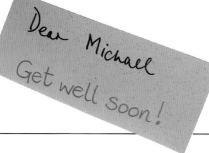

Dear Michael
Get well soon!

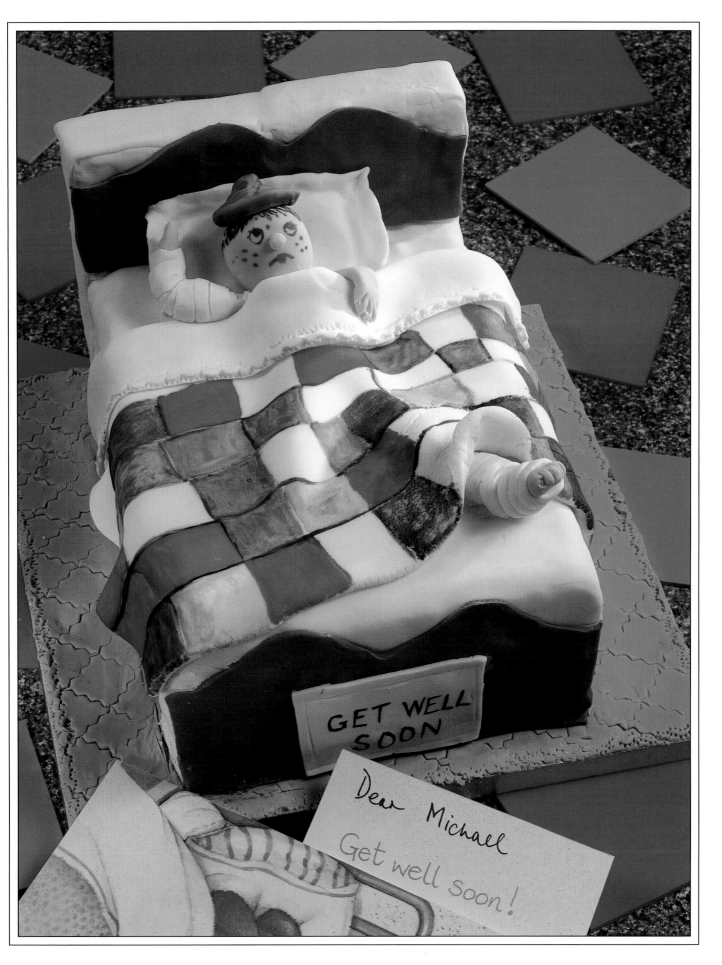

QUICK CRIMPING
AND EMBOSSING

■ ● ▲

Crimping and embossing are two of the simplest techniques to use on fondant iced or marzipan-coated cakes, yet they can produce stunning patterns and decorative effects. Crimpers, or nippers or clippers, are small tweezer-like pieces of equipment, which are squeezed gently into the fondant to make a pattern. Embossers are 'stamps' with a reversed pattern or message, that are simply pressed into the icing to leave an attractive indented image.

A festive Christmas cake has been created using a range of appropriate crimpers. Holly-shaped crimpers, in two sizes, were used to create the sprigs around the edge of the cake, and a Christmas-tree shaped crimper was used to impress the tree in the centre. The shapes are then cleverly painted in using edible paste food colours and a tiny paintbrush. A scarlet ribbon finishes off the cake perfectly.

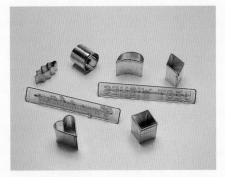

There are about nine types of crimpers and numerous embossers on the market, all available in different patterns. With a selection at your disposal, you can be really creative and produce a number of different effects on a single cake. Be sure to wash them well after use to prevent dried icing clogging the patterns.

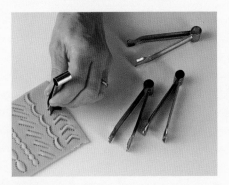

A great range of patterns can be created with crimpers, and they are ideal for making decorative borders and surrounds. Just a few design possibilities are shown on this sample strip of coloured marzipan.

USING EMBOSSERS AND CRIMPERS

First, cover the cake with fondant icing of the required colour and smooth down the sides until they are completely flat. Attach a contrasting ribbon around the base if liked, securing it with a blob of royal icing. Crimp and emboss while the icing is still soft.

1 To emboss a message – here, a 'Happy Birthday' embosser is being used – dip the embosser into icing or confectioner's sugar, then simply press it lightly into the fondant in the desired position.

2 Lift the embosser off carefully, to reveal the impressed image.

3 To crimp a pattern (here overlapping ovals are used), press the crimper into the fondant then pinch it together gently, until the fondant between the tips is about 3 mm (⅛ in) wide. Re-open the crimpers to about 5 mm (¼ in) wide, then lift away; be sure to release the tension on the crimpers as you do this, or you will lift away the fondant

too. Repeat the pattern to make a border all around the cake.

4 Crimp a decorative pattern around the sides of the cake, too, to finish off – here short arcs or curves are crimped into large sweeping loops.

CRIMPING TIPS

To crimp a border around the cake, first pin-prick a line all around the top as a guideline (unless you are sure you can keep a straight line by hand). For easier control of the crimpers, you may wish to put a thick elastic band halfway up the handle, as this stops them opening out completely. Dip the ends of the crimpers regularly in icing or confectioner's sugar as you work to prevent them from sticking to the fondant. Remember, if you do make any mistakes, you can always smooth them over with your finger while the fondant is still soft.

This attractive cake is simply but classically decorated using embossers and crimpers. Swirling loops of scalloped lines wend their way around the top edges and sides of a pale pink fondant-iced cake. A pale pink ribbon completes the effect.

BE MY VALENTINE

A dark-red romantic cake for a loved one which will melt the most prosaic heart.

■ ● ▲

INGREDIENTS

20 cm (8 in) round sponge or chocolate cake
60 ml (4 tbsp) apricot jam, sieved
675 g (1½ lb) fondant icing
red paste food colouring
50 g (2 oz) white royal icing
thin red satin ribbon

1 To shape the cake, trim away two sides, then trim the other two sides, making long sloping cuts, to form a point. Re-position the larger cut pieces at the top of the cake to complete the heart shape. Place the pieces on a 30 cm (12 in) round cake board and brush the joins, top and sides with apricot jam.

3 Colour 450 g (1 lb) fondant bright red. Roll out thinly and drape over the cake. Smooth down the top and sides, then trim very carefully with scissors, avoiding the white frill. Roll out the remaining scraps and cut into a small heart shape. Leave to dry out on waxed paper for 2 hours.

Roll 50 g (2 oz) white fondant into a long thin sausage, and place around the base between the join of the white frill and red fondant.

5 Fill a small greaseproof paper piping bag with royal icing and snip away the tip. Pipe on small dots in a triangular pattern to form a border around the top edge of the cake.

2 Roll out 175 g (6 oz) white fondant thinly to make a long strip. Roll one side with a pastry wheel to give a fluted edge. Take a cocktail stick (toothpick) and roll gently backwards and forwards to flute it into frills. Carefully place the frill around the base of the cake.

4 Using a plastic ruler, mark on a series of spaced lines in one direction, then the other to make a 'quilted' diamond pattern on the top of the cake.

6 Roll out white scraps of fondant into a long thin strip and make another white frill as in step 2, to fit around the small heart-shaped plaque.

Attach the frill under the heart with royal icing. Place in the top right hand corner of the cake and pipe on the message 'Be My Valentine'. Red satin bows add the finishing touch.

EASTER BONNET

With its twisted hatband, crisp bow and pretty flowers, this will be the smartest piece of millinery of the year. Serve it for tea on Easter Sunday, before you start on the chocolate Easter eggs.

■ ● ▲

INGREDIENTS

20 cm (8 in) round sponge or fruit cake
1.8 kg (3½ lb) fondant icing
550 g (1¼ lb) almond paste, for fruit cake
60 ml (4 tbsp) apricot jam, sieved
yellow, purple and orange paste food colourings
purple dusting powder
fine floristry wire
scrap of cream tulle material
fine pale yellow satin ribbon

1 Soften a generous 1.3 kg (3 lb) fondant and colour pale yellow. Colour 225 g (8 oz) fondant purple and store in a plastic bag. Dab a 35 cm (14 in) cake board with apricot jam and brush the rest over the top and sides of the cake. If using a fruit cake, cover with almond paste and leave to dry for 48 hours.

Roll out 450 g (1 lb) of the yellow fondant thinly and cover the cake board. Trim the edges and roll flat. Roll out another 675 g (1½ lb) to a round large enough to cover the cake. Drape the fondant loosely in position and flute up the edges. Smooth down the sides with both hands. Trim away the edges and smooth over any air bubbles. Place the cake in the centre of the board.

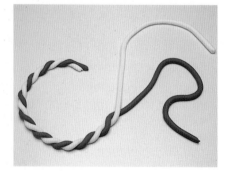

2 To make the twist, roll 100 g (4 oz) each of yellow and purple fondant into two thin ropes long enough to go around the cake. Twist together loosely, then wrap around the base of the cake.

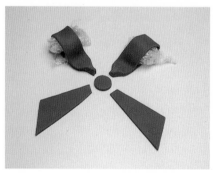

3 To make the bow, roll out 100 g (4 oz) purple fondant and cut into thick oblong strips. Loop two strips over crumpled cling wrap into bow shapes, Cut out a centre button and two bow ends (as shown) and allow to dry out for 2–3 hours to harden.

4 To make 8–10 flowers from 50 g (2 oz) yellow fondant, mould a small ball into a flattened-out nail shape. Use a large blossom cutter to stamp out a flower. Take a cocktail stick (toothpick) and roll around the edge to make a frill. Paint the centre pale orange, dust the edges with a paint brush dipped in purple dusting powder.

5 Make the decoration by wrapping wire around the centre of the tulle, working in loops of ribbon.

6 Position the bow on the cake, attach the tulle bow and place the button on top. Position the flowers on the bonnet.

HALLOWE'EN GHOST

This effective ghost is one of the easiest and quickest cakes to make, and will delight children of all ages. He's so delicious he won't be haunting the house for long when he appears on 31 October, or the eve of All Saints' Day.

■ ● ▲

INGREDIENTS

2 sponge or fruit cakes baked in 800 g (1 lb 15 oz) fruit tins
60 ml (4 tbsp) apricot jam, sieved
450 g (1 lb) almond paste, for fruit cake
700 g (good 1½ lb) white fondant
2 chocolate finger biscuits
black paste food colouring

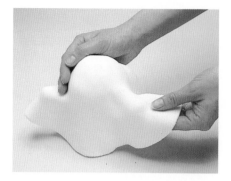

1 Cut the top of one cake completely flat. Cut a rounded shape on the other one. Brush the join, top and sides with apricot jam and sandwich together. If using a fruit cake, cover with almond paste and leave to dry out for 48 hours.

Roll out 175 g (6 oz) white fondant thinly into an oblong strip and wrap around the sides of the cake (as shown).

3 Roll out 450 g (1 lb) white fondant into a 20 cm (8 in) round and drape over the ghost. Smooth down the top and flute up the edges.

Colour 25 g (1 oz) fondant black and cut out eyes and a mouth. Moisten and then stick on the ghost. Place the ghost on a 25 cm (10 in) round cake board covered in black paper, and decorate with a moon and stars cut from scraps.

2 Roll out 50 g (2 oz) white fondant thinly and cover two-thirds of each chocolate biscuit to form the ghost's arms. Push the uncovered ends of the biscuits into the cake, about a third of the way down as shown.

FIREWORKS

1 Brush the cake all over with apricot jam and place on a 25 cm (10 in) square cake board. Colour 550 g (1¼ lb) fondant orange. Roll out thinly and drape over the cake. Smooth the top and sides flat. Trim away excess edges and smooth down again. Roll out the trimmings into four trianglar shapes, 20 cm (8 in) long. Stick the shapes to the top edge of the cake.

Colour 350 g (12 oz) fondant blue and roll out four oblongs 6 × 21 cm (2½ × 8½ in). Decorate the blue oblongs with orange stars and fireworks and stick to the sides of the cake.

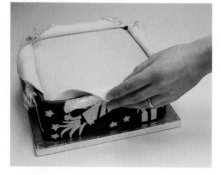

2 Crumple up some cling wrap and fold the triangular lids over. Leave to dry out for 2 hours to harden.

For a sparkling celebration, try this colourful box of fireworks. They're the safest fireworks you can offer and they won't cause any damage – except to the waistline.

■ ● ▲

INGREDIENTS

20 cm (8 in) deep square sponge cake
90 ml (6 tbsp) apricot jam, sieved
1.3 kg (3 lb) fondant icing
orange, blue, red, yellow and green paste food colourings
2 wooden skewers

3 To make the catherine wheels, colour 50 g (2 oz) fondant purple and 50 g (2 oz) orange. Roll out into two long thin sausages and wind up together. Make two catherine wheels.

4 To make the star fountains, colour 75 g (3 oz) fondant green and roll into two pyramids. Colour 25 g (1 oz) yellow and roll into a long sausage. Drape around the pyramids. Make two yellow flames to finish.

5 To make the stick fireworks, colour 75 g (3 oz) fondant red and shape into three sausages. Use 25 g (1 oz) orange scraps to make into small fluted rounds and insert into the top of the fireworks. Trim with stamped out stars.

6 To make the rockets, colour 75 g (3 oz) blue and mould into two stick shapes with small twists for touch paper. Mould 25 g (1 oz) orange scraps into a long rope and twist around the blue sticks. Insert wooden skewers. Arrange the fireworks on top of the cake.

CHRISTMAS

■ ● ▲

I'm sure everyone has attempted to ice a Christmas cake at one time or other, usually using just the traditional white royal icing. The unusual and colourful cakes that follow are not that much more complicated to make if you follow the steps, and they are bound to bring you lots more compliments than a plain cake! Everyone will enjoy the festive Santa on the Christmas Eve *cake, and the cake for* Snowballing Snowmen. *The cakes for a* Christmas Pudding *and* Presents for Everyone *are quick and easy to make, and for special centrepieces, keep the Christmas spirit alive with a* Cookie Tree *or a charming* Gingerbread House.

CHRISTMAS PUDDING

1 Trim the top of the cake flat if it has peaked, turn it upside down and place on a 25 cm (10 in) round cake board. Brush the cake all over with apricot jam. If using a fruit cake, cover with almond paste, then leave to dry out for 48 hours.

2 Colour 550 g (1¼ lb) fondant brown. Roll out thinly and drape over the cake. Smooth down the sides and trim away excess edges and smooth again.

Colour 100 g (4 oz) fondant pale cream with the yellow paste colour and roll out roughly for the custard. Mould any edges smoothly to represent running custard, and place the finished shape over the top of the cake.

This Christmas pudding is so quick and easy to decorate – even if you've been kept working until late on Christmas Eve, there's still time to make it ready for the big day.

■ ● ▲

INGREDIENTS

sponge, fruit or chocolate cake baked in a
1 ltr (1¾ pt) pudding basin
90 ml (6 tbsp) apricot jam, sieved
450 g (1 lb) almond paste for fruit cake
800 g (1¾ lb) fondant icing
brown, yellow, green and red paste
food colourings
icing sugar, for dusting

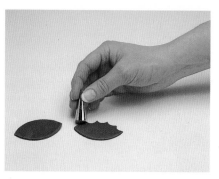

3 Colour 100 g (4 oz) fondant holly green and roll out thinly. Cut out 15 oval shapes, then stamp away the edges with an icing tube to make the leaves spiked. Mark on veins with a knife, pinch together and leave to dry out for 2 hours to harden.

Colour 15 g (½ oz) fondant red and shape into holly berries. Dry out for 2 hours to harden.

4 Position the holly and berries on top of and around the pudding. Dust the cake lightly with icing sugar.

CHRISTMAS EVE

A rather sooty Santa emerges from the chimney to find a welcome offering – a festive glass of sherry.

■ ● ▲

INGREDIENTS

20 cm (8 in) square fruit cake
90 ml (6 tbsp) apricot jam, sieved
800 g (1¾ lb) almond paste
2.25 kg (5 lb) fondant icing
cream, black, brown, red, pink and green
paste food colourings
thin red satin ribbon

1 To shape the cake, cut two slices 2.5 cm (1 in) wide from one side of the cake. Cut 5 cm (2 in) off one slice for the hearth. Cut out an arch for the fireplace about 2.5 cm (1 in) deep into the cake.

Colour 225 g (8 oz) fondant light green and use it to cover a 30 cm (12 in) cake board.

2 Stand the cake upright on its side on the board. Brush the cake all over with apricot jam, then cover with almond paste and leave to dry out for 48 hours. Colour 900 g (2 lb) fondant cream. Roll out thinly and drape over the cake, covering all the sides.

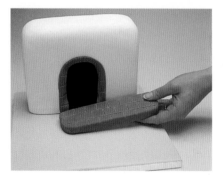

3 Colour 25 g (1 oz) fondant black and roll out thinly. Press into the back of the fireplace. Colour 10 g (4 oz) fondant brown, brush the spare cake pieces with jam and cover with the fondant. Mark on tiles with a knife. Use trimmings to outline the fireplace arch; mark on tiles.

4 To make Santa, colour 400 g (14 oz) fondant red. Mould a hat from 15 g (½ oz) red, roll 15 g (½ oz) pink fondant into a head and make a beard by crinkling 15 g (½ oz) white fondant. Attach a white bobble and trim to the hat, place on the head and stick on the beard and moustache.

5 To make the body, mould 100 g (4 oz) red fondant into a round shape and into two thin sausages for the arms. Trim with 25 g (1 oz) white fondant as shown and make two pink hands from scraps of fondant.

6 To make the legs, roll 75 g (3 oz) red fondant into a sausage and bend in the centre. Shape boots from 40 g (1½ oz) black fondant and place over bottom half of legs. Trim the top of the boots with 15 g (½ oz) white fondant. For the soot, lightly flick black food colouring onto the figure using a wide paintbrush.

7 To decorate the board and fireplace, colour 50 g (2 oz) dark green and roll out for the rug, stamp out patterns and mark the fringing with a cocktail stick (toothpick). Colour 25 g (1 oz) fondant grey and shape into a cat. Roll out 50 g (1 oz) red fondant thinly and cut out two stockings. Add a white trim to each stocking and stick to the chimney with a little water.

To make the swag, colour 75 g (3 oz) fondant green, roll out into two thin sausages and twist together. Suspend across the chimney breast. Shape 50 g (2 oz) red fondant into bows and flute the edges of each with a cocktail stick (toothpick). Stick over each end of the swagging.

Colour 75 g (3 oz) fondant dark brown and make into logs. Use the satin ribbon to decorate the fondant parcel.

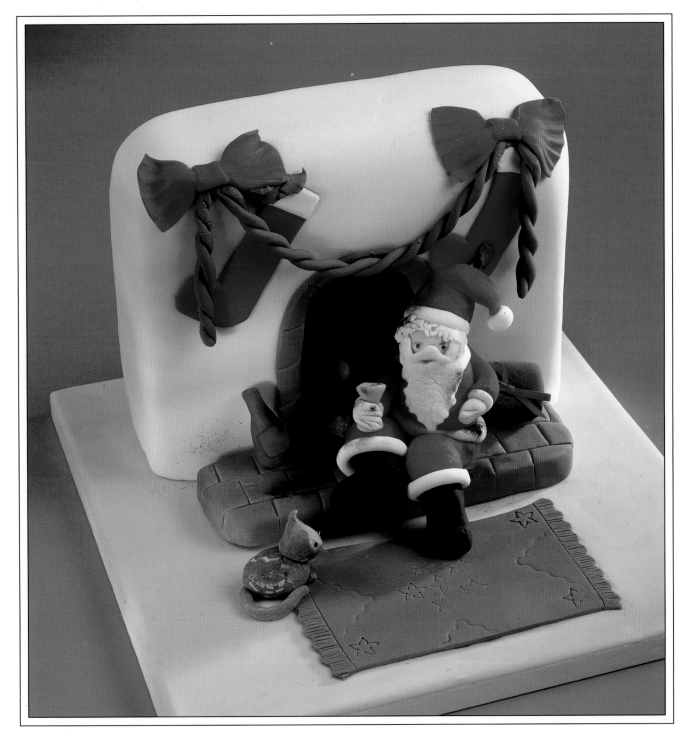

COOKIE TREE

1 Cream the butter and sugar together in a bowl, then beat in the eggs. Stir in the flour and cornflour and knead to a smooth dough. Wrap in foil and chill for 2–3 hours.

Set the oven to 190°C (375°F) Gas 5.

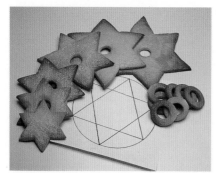

2 Roll out the dough to 0.75 cm (⅓ in) thickness and cut out a 23 cm (9 in), 20 cm (8 in), 18 cm (7 in), 15 cm (6 in), 12.5 cm (5 in) and 10 cm (4 in) star. Stamp out a 2.5 cm (1 in) hole in the centre of all but one of the stars. Stamp 24 × 5 cm (2 in) rounds with a 2.5 cm (1 in) hole in the centre.

Place on greased baking sheets. Bake for 15–20 minutes for the larger pieces, less for the smaller ones. Cool on a wire rack until cold and stiffened.

This Christmas cookie tree is baked from biscuit dough and makes an attractive centrepiece. It is ideal to make for a social club or a school during the festive season.

■ ● ▲

INGREDIENTS

250 g (9 oz) butter, at room temperature
250 g (9 oz) caster sugar
2 eggs, size 2, beaten
450 g (1 lb) plain flour
30 ml (2 tbsp) cornflour

DECORATION

450 g (1 lb) white royal icing
100 g (4 oz) desiccated coconut
30 × 1 cm (12 × ½ in) piece of wooden dowelling
100 g (4 oz) green fondant icing
50 g (2 oz) royal icing, coloured bright red
thin red ribbon

3 Cover the stars and circles with white royal icing, then sprinkle with desiccated coconut. Secure the dowelling base with royal icing on to a 25 cm (10 in) cake board covered with green paper. Layer the stars and circles on the dowelling, as in the picture, starting with the largest star at the base.

4 Roll out the green fondant and stamp out small green holly leaves. Stick two to each point of the star. Pipe on red holly berries with royal icing.

Drape the red ribbon around the cake.

To make the stars you will need stiff card and a pair of compasses. on the card, using the compasses; draw six circles: one 23 cm, one 20 cm, one 18 cm, one 15 cm, one 12.5 cm and one 10 cm. Make each circle into a star as follows.

1 Mark on three equal points with the compass.

2 Draw lines between the points. Repeat the process, drawing in another three points equally between the first ones.

3 Draw in lines again to make a star. Make a 2.5 cm hole in the centre and cut out.

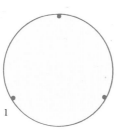
1

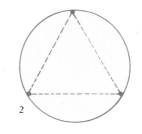
2

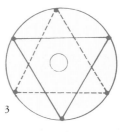
3

SWEET IDEAS

■ ● ▲

If you are looking for a way to decorate a cake in a lively and
unusual way, but without the bother of elaborate piping or fancy
sugarpaste moulding, all you need to do is buy a selection of bright sweets
and candies. There are countless possibilities – a few scattered chocolate
drops or coloured jelly beans for a young child, simple pictures created from
coloured sweets, or abstract patterns with shape and colour. Or, for a
deliciously sophisticated cake, you could cover a cake in white, plain and
milk chocolate truffles and pralines.

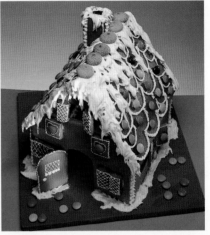

This highly appealing gingerbread house has been decorated with children in mind, using little biscuits and sweets. A traditional gingerbread house (see recipe on page 100) is first decorated with piped white royal icing, both as roof decorations and flicked on to create a snow effect. Then, ratafia biscuits and sugar-coated chocolate beans (Smarties or M&Ms) are added to the roof, each secured with a tiny blob of royal icing.

A simple rectangular sponge cake is transformed into a pirate's treasure chest with coloured sweets. First cover the cake in buttercream, to provide a soft but smooth base for the candies. Then press the sweets in to create the design: here, chocolate buttons have been used for the 'wood trim', and more elaborate chocolate shapes for the chain and lock. Then, multi-coloured sweets and jellies of all kinds have been used to fill in the main areas.

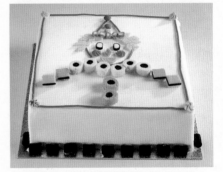

A smiling clown face has been created out of candies, on a simple white fondant-iced square cake. Liquorice sweets have been used to make up the body, buttons and coloured jellies the features of the face and hair. Use liquorice shoelaces to form the outline of the face, and as a border to the cake. Use your imagination to create your very own personal character!

GINGERBREAD HOUSE

1 Line four rigid baking sheets with non-stick paper. Set the oven to 180°C (350°F) gas 4. Copy the templates below onto card and cut out.

Melt the golden syrup or honey in a small pan or in the microwave. Beat the butter and sugar in a bowl until light and fluffy, then beat in the egg yolks, one at a time. Sift in the flour, bicarbonate of soda, spices and cocoa and fold in with a spoon. Add the syrup or honey and enough milk to make a soft, but not sticky, dough. Knead until the dough is smooth.

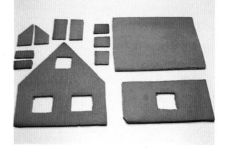

2 Roll out the dough between two sheets of non-stick paper to about 0.5 cm (¼ in) thick. Cut out the pieces using the templates and lift them carefully onto the baking sheets (use a fish slice to help). Bake for 10–12 minutes, then allow to cool on the sheets to harden. Check the shapes against the templates and trim to shape while still warm, if necessary. Leave the pieces on a wire rack until firm enough to handle, about 4–5 hours.

A gingerbread house is a fun and simple cake to make for Christmas. You'll be rewarded both by the wonderful aromas that fill the house during the baking, and by the looks of wonder from the children when you bring it finished to the table.

■ ● ▲

INGREDIENTS

90 ml (3 tbsp) golden syrup or honey
175 g (6 oz) butter
175 g (6 oz) muscovado sugar
3 yolks from size 3 eggs
675 g (1½ lb) plain flour
7.5 ml (1½ tsp) bicarbonate of soda
10 ml (2 tsp) ground ginger
5 ml (1 tsp) mixed spice
15 ml (1 tbsp) cocoa powder, sifted
135–150 ml (9–10 tbsp) milk
900 g (2 lb) royal icing
ratafia biscuits
Smarties (M & Ms)

3 Take the two fronts and two sides of the house, stick the bases to a 35 cm (14 in) square cake board with royal icing and join the side walls. Leave to dry out until rigid.

4 Stick the two roof sections together then stick on to the house. Stick on the window shutters and door. Leave to dry out until solid.

5 With royal icing, pipe fine lattice work on the door and some of the shutters, then using a larger tube, pipe on the roof decorations. Stick on the chimney pieces and leave to dry out, piping in between the joins.

Flick remaining royal icing over the roof, chimney and cake board to represent snow, and decorate the roof with ratafia biscuits and Smarties.

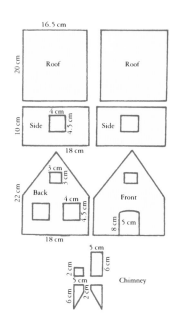

SNOWBALLING SNOWMEN

You can have lots of fun with these snowmen. Experiment with your own variations on this snowy scene.

■ ● ▲

INGREDIENTS

20 cm (8 in) square sponge or fruit cake
60 ml (4 tbsp) apricot jam, sieved
800 g (1¾ lb) almond paste, for fruit cake
1.85 kg (4¼ lb) fondant icing
green, brown, red, blue, yellow, black and orange paste food colourings
piece of string

1 Brush the cake all over with apricot jam. If using a fruit cake, cover with almond paste, then leave to dry out for 48 hours. Mould 175 g (6 oz) white fondant into hills and ski slopes and position on the cake. Place the cake on a 25 cm (10 in) square cake board.

Roll out 800 g (1¾ lb) white fondant and drape over the shapes and top and sides of cake. Smooth down with the palms of your hands. Trim excess edges and smooth down the sides again. Re-roll trimmings and make about 55 small snowballs. Leave to dry out for 2 hours.

2 To make the Christmas trees, colour 450 g (1 lb) fondant green and shape into four pyramids. Snip with scissors to represent foliage.

Colour 25 g (1 oz) fondant brown, shape into sausages and chop into trunks for the Christmas trees.

3 To make the snowmen, mould 175 g (6 oz) white fondant into the heads and bodies. Mould 25 g (1 oz) red fondant and 25 g (1 oz) blue fondant into scarfs and hats. Trim the hats and scarfs with 15 g (½ oz) yellow fondant. Mould 25 g (1 oz) black fondant into another hat, and eyes, buttons and mouths. Use 7 g (¼ oz) orange fondant for noses.

4 Mould 25 g (1 oz) brown fondant into a bench and 7 g (¼ oz) grey fondant into a newspaper. Use 15 g (½ oz) black fondant for an umbrella and 25 g (1 oz) brown fondant for a sledge. Press 25 g (1 oz) green fondant through a sieve for grass and stick to the cake. Leave to dry out for 2 hours.

Assemble all the pieces by dampening lightly, then pressing together. Position the pieces on the cake as shown.

CHOCOLATE CHRISTMAS WREATH

1 Wash and dry plenty of spiked and plain holly leaves. Very gently melt the chocolate in three separate bowls standing over a pan of warm water, or in the microwave. Be very careful not to let any steam get into the chocolate or it will 'seize' and become unmanageable. This will also happen if the chocolate becomes overheated, or water gets in.

2 Carefully coat the back of each leaf with melted chocolate and leave to dry out on a plate. Keep the leaves in the refrigerator for 2 hours or overnight, until the chocolate is hardened.

Some people simply don't like fruit cake and marzipan. Here is an alternative which will delight chocoholics, too.

■ ● ▲

INGREDIENTS

20 cm (8 in) round chocolate cake
holly leaves
225 g (8 oz) white chocolate
225 g (8 oz) milk chocolate
225 g (8 oz) plain dark chocolate
basic buttercream icing with 40 g
(1½ oz) cooled, melted plain
chocolate added

3 Carefully peel away the holly leaves from the chocolate. The top of the chocolate leaves will be left with the impression of the holly veins. Keep the leaves chilled until needed.

4 Using a mug or teacup as a guide, cut a central hole out of the cake to form a ring shape. Trim the edges, so that they slope. Place the cake on a 25 cm (10 in) round cake board and cover with three-quarters of the chocolate buttercream. Place the remaining quarter in a piping bag fitted with a large star tube and pipe lines across the cake to represent twigs.

Place the chocolate leaves on the cake, alternating the colours and keep chilled in the refrigerator until needed.

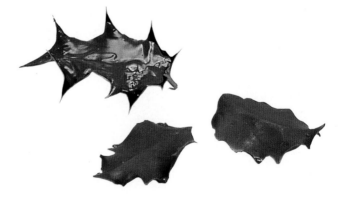

PRESENTS FOR EVERYONE

1 Trim the top from the cake if it has peaked. Turn the cake over and brush all over with apricot jam.

2 Colour 550 g (1¼ lb) fondant brown. Roll out 50 g (2 oz) thinly and use to cover the smaller top end. Roll 25 g (1 oz) into a sausage and position to make a raised edge around the top.

Roll out the remaining brown

Even if you've never made a cake before, do try this one. It is the simplest Christmas cake ever, and you can experiment making all different kinds of coloured presents.

■ ● ▲

INGREDIENTS

sponge cake cooked in a 1 ltr (1¾ pt) pudding basin or 800 g (2 lb) fruit tin 60 ml (4 tbsp) apricot jam, sieved 900 g (2 lb) fondant icing brown, cream, red, blue, purple and green paste food colourings thin satin ribbons

fondant into a round with a diameter of 35 cm (12–14 in). Sit the cake in the centre and gather up the sides, pleating together around the top edges. Trim away the top edges if too full. Position the cake on a 20 cm (8 in) round covered cake board.

Colour 50 g (2 oz) fondant cream, roll into a sausage to make a cord. Wrap the cord under the top of the sack and make a bow at the back.

3 Colour 225 g (8 oz) fondant into assorted colours, then mould into square, round, oblong and sausage shaped presents. Twist 15 g (½ oz) each of red and white fondant together to make walking sticks. Leave the presents to dry out for 2 hours, then decorate with ribbons. Place the presents in the top of the sack and around the base. Decorate the board with cut-outs, using scraps of coloured fondant.

USEFUL INFORMATION

The recipes in this book give ingredients in metric and imperial
measures. It is important to follow only one set of measures,
and never to mix them, as they are not exact quantities.
The tables below show the equivalents used in this book.
All spoon measures are level.

OVEN TEMPERATURE CHART

	°C	°F	Gas Mark
Very cool	140	275	1
Cool	150	300	2
Warm	160	325	3
Moderate	180	350	4

LENGTHS

Metric	Imperial
2 cm	¾ in
2.5 cm	1 in
3 cm	1¼ in
4 cm	1½ in
4.5 cm	1¾ in
5 cm	2 in
6 cm	2¼–½ in
7.5 cm	3 in
8 cm	3¼ in
10 cm	4 in
12 cm	5 in
15 cm	6 in
16.5 cm	6½ in
18 cm	7 in
20 cm	8 in
22 cm	8½ in
23 cm	9 in
25 cm	10 in
28 cm	11 in
30 cm	12 in
35 cm	14 in

LIQUIDS

Metric	Imperial
1.25 ml	¼ tsp
2.5 ml	½ tsp
5 ml	1 tsp
7.5 ml	1½ tsp
10 ml	2 tsp
12.5 ml	2½ tsp
15 ml	1 tbsp
22.5 ml	1½ tbsp
30 ml	2 tbsp
45 ml	3 tbsp (2 fl oz)
50 ml	3½ tbsp
60 ml	4 tbsp
90 ml	6 tbsp (4 fl oz)
120 ml	8 tbsp
1 ltr	1¾ pt

DRY INGREDIENTS

Metric	Imperial
7 g	¼ oz
15 g	½ oz
25 g	1 oz
40 g	1½ oz
50 g	2 oz
75 g	3 oz
100 g	4 oz
150 g	5 oz
175 g	6 oz
200 g	7 oz
225 g	8 oz
250 g	9 oz
275 g	10 oz
350 g	12 oz
400 g	14 oz
450 g	1 lb
500 g	1 lb 2 oz
550 g	1 lb 4 oz
600 g	1 lb 5 oz
675 g	1 lb 8 oz
800 g	1 lb 12 oz
900 g	2 lb
1 kg	2 lb 4 oz
1.15 kg	2 lb 8 oz
1.2 kg	2 lb 12 oz
1.3 kg	3 lb
1.5 kg	3 lb 2 oz
1.75 kg	4 lb
1.85 kg	4 lb 4 oz
2.5 kg	5 lb 8 oz

GLOSSARY

ALMOND PASTE: almond icing.

BICARBONATE OF SODA: baking soda, an ingredient of baking powder. It must be measured accurately as too much bicarbonate of soda will give a poor result and a bitter aftertaste.

BUTTER: gives better flavour and texture than margarine in cake making.
UNSALTED BUTTER: gives better results than salted, in baking.

BUTTERCREAM ICING: Vienna cream icing. See page 11 for recipe.

COCONUT, DESICCATED: finely shredded dried coconut.

CORNFLOUR: cornstarch.

FONDANT ICING: made from liquid glucose, egg white and icing sugar, it is also known as plastic icing or soft icing. See page 12 for recipe.
TO STICK FONDANT ICING: fondant icing will adhere easily. Brush lightly with boiled water or with a clear spirit, such as gin, and position.

GINGER, GROUND: powdered ginger, a strongly pungent spice.

GLACÉ FRUITS: crystallized fruits coated with a heavy sugar syrup and allowed to dry.

GOLDEN SYRUP: maple or pancake syrup can be substituted.

GLYCERINE: a sweet colourless syrup, sold in bottles from chemists and/or health food stores. Helps to retain moisture in cake icing and prevents excessive hardening.

ICING SUGAR: confectioner's or powdered sugar. This white sugar is very fine and powdery. Keep it in a dry place and always sift before use as it tends to form lumps in storage.

JAM: conserve.

LIQUID GLUCOSE (GLUCOSE SYRUP): made from wheat starch, it is available from health food stores and supermarkets.

MARGARINE: good quality cooking margarine (or polyunsaturated margarine for the cholesteral-conscious) may be used in cake making in place of butter.

MIXED PEEL: a mixture of crystallized citrus peel.

MIXED SPICE: (not to be confused with allspice) a finely ground combination of spices, which include nutmeg, ginger, allspice (pimento) and cinnamon, used for flavouring fruit cakes.

PLAIN FLOUR: all-purpose flour.

RAISINS: dried, dark sweet grapes.

RATAFIA BISCUITS: small round macaroon biscuits from Italy.

RICE CRISPIES: rice bubbles.

SELF-RAISING FLOUR: this has raising agents already mixed into it. If a recipe calls for self-raising flour and you have none, use all-purpose flour with baking powder added in the proportion of 250 g (9 oz) to 12.5 ml (2½ teaspoons) baking powder. Sift several times before using.

SMARTIES: M & Ms or any small round coloured sweets.

SUGAR:
CASTER SUGAR: fine, white granulated sugar. It creams easily with butter and dissolves quickly into the mixture.
SOFT BROWN SUGAR: this creams well with butter, and is mostly used in fruit cake recipes, where rich flavour and colour are needed.
MUSCOVADO SUGAR: this is the best soft dark brown sugar, as it is naturally unrefined and has an excellent rich flavour and dark colour.

SUGARPASTE: also known as Continental fondant icing; see page 12 for recipe.

SULTANAS: seedless white raisins.

TREACLE, DARK: molasses can be substituted.

VANILLA ESSENCE: imitation vanilla essence may be used.

EQUIPMENT

BASKETWEAVE: an icing nozzle that forms a basketweave pattern.

CAN, CANNED: tin, tinned.

CLING WRAP: plastic wrap.

COCKTAIL STICKS: toothpicks.

DAISY CUTTER: a flower cutter shaped to resemble a daisy.

FLORISTRY WIRE: a thin, flexible wire used in flower decorating, which is coated with green or white paper.

FOIL: aluminium foil.

FRUIT TIN (CAN): a tin (can) that has contained canned fruit (don't use tins that have contained other foods; tuna, for example, leaves an odour that is hard to wash out). Once emptied, the tin (can) should be thoroughly washed and dried ready for use in baking – it is the ideal shape for tall round cakes.

GREASEPROOF PAPER: waxproof paper.

NON-STICK SILICONE PAPER: a paper that has been coated with silicone, it provides a nonstick surface for lining cake tins.

PALETTE KNIFE: spatula-like knife for smoothing icing; to get a really smooth finish, dip the knife in hot water first.

INDEX